The Beverly Hills Organizer's
Home Organizing Bible

The Beverly Hills Organizer's

Home Organizing Bible

A Pro's Answers
to Your Organizing Prayers

Linda Koopersmith

The Beverly Hills Organizer

FAIR WINDS
PRESS
GLOUCESTER, MASSACHUSETTS

Text © 2005 by Linda Koopersmith
Photographs © 2005 by Myk Mishoe

First published in the USA in 2005 by
Fair Winds Press
33 Commercial Street
Gloucester, MA 01930

08 07 06 05 04 1 2 3 4 5

ISBN 1-59233-154-8

Library of Congress Cataloging-in-Publication
Data available

Cover design by Joanna Detz
Cover photographs Courtesy of California
Closets/www.californiaclosets.com
Cover portrait by Myk Mishoe
Book design by Joanna Detz
Interior Photographs by Myk Mishoe except
where noted
Hair by Lawrence Davis and Image by Kimarie
Makeup by Bonni Flowers
Styling by Chase Koopersmith
Printed and bound in Singapore

CONTENTS

* * * * * *

Looking back, I can see that I was born to organize. I was the youngest of three children, two girls and one boy. Unfortunately for my sister, I was a girl, which meant that she would be forced to give up half of her bedroom space after seven years of single occupancy. In retrospect, I have to say, this is a tough move for anyone, especially when your new room-mate is a crying baby. As we grew older, my sister and I began to act like Felix and Oscar from the old television series *The Odd Couple*. It was plain to see from the beginning that I took on the role of Felix, the neat and tidy one.

After I graduated from college, I moved to Los Angeles. I was involved with many different businesses. My most prominent career, in commercial real estate, led me to consider organization. I remember walking into an office space and seeing snowdrifts of paper. Two thoughts occurred to me: first, that the room could be downsized if the papers were organized in files (saving rent money), and second, that more profit could be made if they were organized (no more wasted time searching for needed documents).

I spent three years leasing real estate before I was ready for a change. At the time, a close friend of mine, who was an interior designer, found her life in shambles. She had gotten divorced after a fourteen-year marriage, during which her husband had handled all of her personal and business affairs. My friend desperately needed to hire someone to get her life in order, and I volunteered for the job. I spent four months piecing her life back together, including arranging her papers, bills, and closets, and even a storage unit. All of it needed to be organized. After this experience, I knew what my purpose was. It was, and still is, to help others become organized.

I have spent the past fifteen years of my life working as a professional organizer, and I have worked for and twelve of them as a seminar leader on the subject. I have seen it all firsthand. I know the problem areas and concerns, and I'm here to help you get through each and every one of them.

You might be wondering what the secret is behind those beautifully organized rooms on the pages of your favorite design magazines. How do the owners do it? They must have a staff of people working for them and no spouses or children around messing things up, or maybe they don't even live there, right? Wrong!

You—yes, you—can have the home you have always dreamed of. All it takes is making the time commitment and following the steps on the pages of this book. As you tackle each part of your house, going through the piles, stacks, and junk, it will be like I am working beside you. Who knows, along the way you may discover some long-forgotten treasures. At the end, your home will be your showplace.

Whether you are a packrat or just need a few tweaks around your home, this book will help you achieve your organizational goals. In this book, I address how to organize every room in the house and beyond. Now the only question is, what are you waiting for?

KEEP AT IT—AND IT *WILL* HAPPEN!

The biggest misconception with organization is that it is a one-shot deal. Many people begin every January 1 with the New Year's resolution, "I'm going to get organized this year." They pick a weekend to pull everything out of their drawers and closets, and they either become overwhelmed or burnt out! What happens next is the traditional "shove it back in the drawers and under the bed so no one will see it" event. This cycle never ends, and the house remains disorganized until the next year, when the cycle occurs again.

The solution? Organization *must* be incorporated into your daily activities. If you decided to run a marathon, could you make it to the finish line without training for it first? Of course not! You would suffer from fatigue before you had gone a mile, and you might never attempt a marathon again. Organizing needs to be approached like an exercise routine. Build up to it slowly by starting with simple tasks that take only fifteen to twenty minutes, then stop.

You can continue with these tasks three to four times a day if you can find the time, but don't take longer than twenty minutes at a time. As you begin to progress, give yourself a little more time, twenty to thirty minutes, and so on. Let's do the math: 20 minutes × 3 times a day × 1 week = 7 hours of organizing. You will witness results, feel like it took no time at all, and enjoy the lifestyle change. These changes will motivate you to continue on the path to organization nirvana. Remember, it takes time to get organized. You do not go into a gym one time and walk out with Arnold's muscles. Do not expect miracles overnight.

If every room of your home is a mess, it may take six months or more to dig your way out of the clutter. Please don't be discouraged! Getting organized and decluttering is like losing weight, and it is impossible to lose fifty pounds in a weekend or even a month. Your disorganization weight will drop off, and at the end you will uncover a whole new home. A whole new world! So what are you waiting for? Let's get started!

PART ONE

* * * * *

Getting Started

Chapter 1

What You'll Need to Succeed

The first hurdle to overcome in setting out to achieve your organizing goals is to realize that organization is a lifestyle. It is not a "do and be done" type of accomplishment, like building a house or graduating from school. Instead, you are starting out on a new path—a way of life that eliminates stress, frees up your time, and satisfies your need to live in an orderly fashion. Like any major change that you set out to achieve, there may be setbacks. The old adages "good things come to those who wait," "patience is a virtue," "cleanliness is next to Godliness," and "Rome wasn't built in a day" should all be part of your new mantra.

Basically, there are just four things you need to get started on your new path to a well-organized home: time, patience, tools, and a fresh eye. Let's look at each of these in turn.

THE FIRST ELEMENT: TIME

It has taken you a lifetime to get to the point where you are today with your clutter. It is an accumulation of all your worldly possessions, gifts, memories, and "junk" you couldn't part with nor find a place to stash. I want you to realize that it will take time to go through all your stuff. Don't get discouraged by the task in front of you. To get started, take one box, bag, or handful at a time out of the cluttered area and bring it into another space. There, you will not be overwhelmed by the magnitude of work in front of you. If your entire home is filled to the gills, clear out a space that you can work in. Clutter is a distraction, and I do not want you to get derailed and sidetracked by your surroundings.

Take the pressure off of yourself now and realize that this job will not be completed in a day. In fact, organizing will become part of your daily activities for the rest of your life.

This isn't a race against the clock to finish by a certain time. Remember, in time, you will be living and working in an organized environment. Imagine what your home will look like once it is organized. Store this picture in the back of your mind and keep moving forward. Each day that you organize a little bit here and there will contribute to the final product, your completely organized home, with everything at your fingertips!

I want you to think about six months from now. Imagine how pleased you will be with all the work you have accomplished around your home and office. Follow my plan, and you will succeed!

The key is to start small. This will keep you from suffering burnout. Pick small tasks to start with and build from there. The best place to start is by organizing drawers. You can finish a drawer in a relatively short amount of time and immediately see your progress. (We'll talk about drawers in detail in Chapter 4.)

I always like to think of organizing in the same way as I think about working out. The way you feel after you've been organizing is very similar to the way you feel after a good workout, and you begin to see the results right away. When the muscle definition begins to come through, you enjoy the new you and work hard to keep the results, and you even try to improve upon them. This will happen with your organizing accomplishments, too.

Keep It Short and Sweet

Start out by organizing for fifteen to twenty minutes at a time. Keep a clock handy or set a timer. When the bell rings, stop. This will do two things for you. It will force you to work on smaller tasks, where you will see immediate results, and it will keep you from doing too much and consequently suffering from fatigue. It doesn't matter if you think you are on a roll. *Stop*! That roll will carry you into a state of burnout, where you will no longer want to work. Take a break. Then, at least two more times during the day, repeat the fifteen- to twenty-minute time frame.

At the end of the day, you will have worked on your organizing for approximately one hour. At the end of the week, you will have accomplished as much as seven hours of work. Can you image how phenomenal things will be at the end of just one month? Your total monthly time invested in organizing will be more than twenty-four hours. That is a full day's work!

As you move through the process and build your stamina level, you can increase the twenty minutes to thirty minutes, and so on. I consider myself a marathon organizer. I can run through a day at full speed for seventeen hours of non-stop organizing. I do not become tired because I have been doing this type of work since 1989, every day. But I'm warning you: Please do *not* try this, because it is inevitable that you will become overwhelmed and might not ever try to organize your home again. If you keep organizing and follow the steps I provide for you, you, too, will eventually be able to organize for longer periods of time.

I remember a sweet, little old lady named Dorothy, who took my seniors' organizing class. Dorothy was in her mid-seventies and eager to get organized. Her entire life was spent chasing the dream, but she was never able to get it together. After taking my seminar, Dorothy had a whole new perspective on organizing. She couldn't wait to dig in and get started.

One day, shortly after the class, I received a phone call from Dorothy. She asked, "Linda, did you know that Staples is open at 3 A.M.?" Shocked that Dorothy had been out buying file folders at that hour, I repeated to her my advice about taking it slow. I warned Dorothy that if she did too much too soon, she would fail. I suggested she get a good night's sleep and that her organizing could keep until the morning. Two weeks later, I got another call from Dorothy. This time she wanted to let me know, "Linda, you were right, I burned out."

People often think this won't happen to them. *Yes it will!* Learn from the mistakes of

Dorothy and others before you. Take it slow, and you will become organized beyond your wildest imagination. Rush into organizing, and it will be the same old story time and time again—pull it all out and shove it back in. Repeat after me (aloud!): "I am going to give myself the time I need to organize my life."

THE SECOND ELEMENT: PATIENCE

Patience is the key element in maintaining all of your hard work. Have you ever spent a weekend organizing your home office, to find that, by Monday morning, a fresh snowfall of white paper covers your desk? Two things are going on when this happens. First, the snowfall of papers that eventually builds up into snowdrifts needs a final resting place, which is where files come in. When each paper, object, or piece of memorabilia doesn't have a place, it's out of place—creating clutter. Second, although the room had been properly organized, the maintenance was ignored.

If the snowdrift scenario has happened to you, it may be for a few reasons. Perhaps nothing has a place, and therefore, you cannot put it away. The place in which you stuff your papers is a mess, too, so you couldn't find a paper later if you tried. Or, after spending time organizing, you started up with your bad habits again by not putting things away. Don't you dare give me that "I have to have everything out in front of me because I have to see it" line! You will have more success in life when you know what you need and where to find it when you need it.

Patience is the key to keeping your space in check. It takes patience to put things back

My Bonus Guarantee

The greatest thing about following my instructions is that as you pursue organizing, you'll find that eventually it turns around and pursues you. You will no longer have to force yourself to get motivated. This is truly the greatest bonus of all. Imagine the day when you automatically put things away in their designated spaces without having to think about it at all.

It even gets better than that! Once everything is in place, you will automatically notice problem areas sticking out at you like sore thumbs and find yourself immediately gravitating to these areas to correct them.

From personal experience, I can validate the fact that I have pursued organization to the point that I no longer have to even think about a task. Organization has become so much a part of my life that it is as natural as breathing. This will happen for you, too, and that is your bonus guarantee!

after you've used them. You have to keep it in the back of your mind at all times. Without this element, all your hard work will eventually fall by the wayside. It would be like taking a year to lose fifty pounds, then suddenly eating everything in sight, packing the weight back on overnight.

Remember this is a new lifestyle; you need to adapt and make the changes to bring your dreams to reality. There will be times that you will slack off. That is okay, too. No one is perfect, and people get busy. However, if you organize properly, everything will have a final resting place when you take the time to maintain your spaces.

THE THIRD ELEMENT: TOOLS

Organizing tools are the secret behind expanding and organizing your space. Without them, you will go nowhere. You will not be any better off than if you went on a road trip without gas in your vehicle. What are tools? In the Gallery of Tools located in the back of this book, beginning on page 178, you will find the treasures that I use to make organizing miracles possible. Some of my favorite organizing tools include china racks, helper shelves, and drawer organizers. Tools are my treasures, because without them, I cannot do my work. I use them to expand space, to create space where there was once none, and to keep items from shifting about and becoming comingled. I also use tools for the aesthetic aspect of a well-organized space.

Tools are the financial investment you will make in getting organized. Most organizing products cost between $10 and $20. Knowing that this could be a substantial cost in your pursuit of organization, it is good to think ahead and make a plan. Depending on the size of your home, you could invest anywhere from $350 to $2,500 in tools. This cost does not completely include customizing your closets, which could cost considerably more if you have them custom-designed.

Even if you don't need to budget to make the investment in tools, do not go out and buy everything you need at once. Remember, you need to pace yourself, starting with small tasks and moving to larger ones. Think of tools like groceries: You will be making several trips to the store as you need them.

Tools and technique must go hand in hand. As you read the organizing "recipes" in the chapters that follow, refer to the Gallery of Tools, beginning on page 178, for your ingredients, and make your shopping list. If you need to, take this book with you to the store. This book is your reference guide for making the right purchases.

THE FOURTH ELEMENT: A FRESH EYE

Having a fresh eye means looking at your space as if it were for the first time. When I enter a home or office, I am looking through the clutter, taking in the space, the configuration, the contents in the room or closet, and surmising from the onset exactly what needs to be done. I can actually see the end result from the first time I walk in to a space. This is a talent that you can develop, too.

When you walk into a space with a fresh eye, go through the contents of the room and make a mental or handwritten inventory. Items that don't belong in the space should be moved out. The items that belong in the room will either have a space created for them, or they will be put away in a proper place that already exists. I think of spaces that have gone wild like toilet paper that has spun off the roll. The once-tidy roll that fit into a small space can expand and take over an entire room. It is your job to untangle the mess and roll it back up. I call this the shrinking process.

If it is too difficult for you to get past the wall of clutter and view your space with a fresh eye, ask some friends to visit and discuss the room with you. It is often easier to look at things with a fresh eye when is not your stuff. Consultations with professional organizers can also help you.

Organizing is like a puzzle: Sometimes after you execute an organizing plan, things just do not fit. When this happens, keep the fresh eye open and make adjustments. Remember that organization is ever-changing, just as we ourselves are. The needs you had yesterday will be different from the needs you will have five years from now.

Now that you know what you need to succeed—time, patience, tools, and a fresh eye—and how to use them, let's go on to my four organizing rules.

Chapter 2

The Rules

Organizing requires structure and ground rules to guide you along the way. My rules are few but powerful. These are the four golden rules that you will incorporate into your daily activities to help you get and stay organized, once and for all.

RULE #1: THE 30-SECOND RULE

My first organizing rule is all about maintaining order so you don't keep spinning into a clutter spiral. Your maintenance routine is simple, and it takes only thirty seconds. If you take something out, off, or in, put it away when you are finished using it, right then and there. Do not put it off! It only takes thirty seconds to keep everything in order and under control.

RULE #2: PILES OF LIKE ITEMS

The most basic rule of organizing is to put all like items together. For example, instead of storing some gardening tools in your basement, others in your garage, and still others in your shed, put them all together. Making piles of like items will now become your way of life. Put everything you have that is "like" together.

When you go through the organizing projects in this book, usually one of the first steps is to sort things, putting like items together. One reason we do this is so that you can see how many you own of that particular item. I worked with a client who had twenty-nine toenail clippers! Of course, the family had no idea they had that many clippers, because when they needed one, they could not find it. This forced them to purchase another clipper. It was not until we gathered the items in their home and sorted them into piles of like items that they realized the gross amount they had purchased. I'm sure my client had spent at least $50 on extra clippers.

Imagine how much money you will save when you get organized. Repeat purchasing will be a part of your past. Just think of the peace of mind you will have once everything has a place and you can find it when you need it.

Once the sorting process is complete, you can determine where these items will be placed and what size tool (such as a basket, crate, or shelf) you need to purchase to contain them.

RULE #3:
REDUCE, REUSE, RECYCLE

While you're organizing, a goal to keep in mind is to get rid of anything that is no longer working for you. This doesn't necessarily mean throw it away. You might be able to reuse or recycle it.

The hardest part of organizing for true diehard packrats is the letting-go process. Let me state here that you can keep everything you ever owned, including your tricycle, if you have a place for it and you know where to find it when you want it. My philosophy is not to throw everything out. But I *do* want you to take a good look at your possessions.

Keep in mind as you sort that different items have different shelf lives. For example, clothing has a two-year life. If you haven't worn a piece of clothing in two years, unless it's a tuxedo or a gown, most likely you will not wear it again. Yes, fashions do return, but not exactly. Fluctuating weight can be another problem.

During the sorting process, you will come across stuff that needs extra thought. These are items that you have been holding onto "just because," or for their sentimental values, or because you might need them someday, or for no reason at all. Try to evaluate each item to the best of your ability. If you still have a problem parting with items you should get rid of, containerize them and move them to a place in which you can store them. Mark your calendar for six months in the future, when you'll revisit the container. Odds are, you will not even think about those items until the date comes up on your calendar. If this is the case, it is a safe bet you can consider donating these items to charity or selling them.

I've found that sentimental items can be a source of anguish. You are dragging around old baggage that no longer has a place in your life, but it has an attachment to your memory. When I approached this subject at one organizing seminar, a sixty-year-old woman named Maggie raised her hand with a comment. Maggie informed the class that she still had all of her maternity clothes and couldn't get rid of them. She had great pregnancies, and she felt that parting with the clothes would be like losing a part of her memories.

A great way to hold onto those memories without keeping the physical possessions is to create a photo album or scrapbook for these items. I suggested to Maggie that she photograph her clothing and perhaps cut swatches of the fabrics from the hemlines. She could put these things into a memory book and part with the clothes. This way, Maggie could still enjoy her fond memories without taking up the space.

For the handy people among us who still cannot part with those sentimental items, you can always choose to recycle pieces. For example, make a quilt out of old clothes, frame favorite old album covers, or create a mosaic with pieces of old china.

Charity is always a great way to let go of belongings and feel good in the process. Choose a charity that will itemize your donation for you and place a value on your items. This will protect you if you are using the donation as a tax deduction.

Another way to pare down your belongings is to have a garage sale. I am a big fan of garage and yard sales. They're a way to eliminate clutter and make money in the process. Sales can offset the cost of a move or simply bring in some extra money. You can use this money to offset the cost of your organizing tools. Remember that your "trash" is another man's (or woman's) treasure.

No matter what choices you make in downsizing the amount of clutter you currently have in your home, it is all part of the organizing process.

RULE #4: NOTHING ON THE FLOOR NO MORE!

The pages of your favorite design magazines all have one thing in common: There's nothing on the floor. Floors are made for walking, not stubbing toes and climbing over piles.

Once you have a firm grip on the fact that a floor is not a big shelf at your feet, you can begin to clear the space. Everything that is lying on the floor needs to be picked up, sorted into like items, and put away.

You do have four walls: Use them! Purchase shelving or bookcases. View your space from the ceiling down. You can use an organizing tool called Rafter Solutions, which we'll talk more about later, to pick up more organizing footage. Whatever your next organizing choices will be, from now on, you will not be setting stuff on the floor!

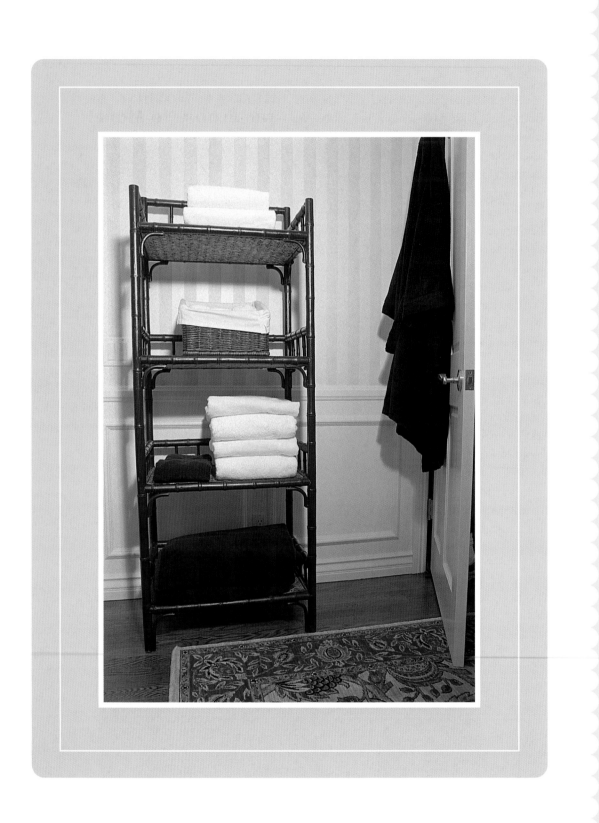

Chapter 3

Where to Begin

Getting started can be so overwhelming and confusing that it can keep you from actually diving in. I've found that, for many people, starting to organize can be stressful. You may find yourself doing one of several things: Aimlessly moving about from one place to another, losing concentration, becoming distracted by the items you uncover, and/or feeling anxiety and fatigue. Those reactions are completely normal. While working with my clients, I am constantly reeling them back into the reality of what we are undertaking. It is very easy to throw up barriers when you are in the beginning stages of organizing. Staying with the plan you set for the space will keep you on track.

TOOL UP

When beginning an organizing project, I like to start small, such as with a drawer or a small closet. Once you determine the area in which you will begin, make a list of the tools you will need for the job. (In this book, I include a list of tools at the beginning of each organizing "recipe.") Just as a contractor cannot build a home without lumber and nails, you cannot get organized without your tools. Don't even think you are going to succeed without them! It will not work.

The organizing tools I recommend in this book have all been selected by me after many years of experience. I consider these products to be the best available in the marketplace today. These products will become part of your life. Make it your business to study the new items that become available each year. Does the product make sense to you? Will it work in your space? Learn to enjoy the process; after all, it's fun to shop!

Get a Labeler!

One tool you need when you start your organizing tasks is a labeler. I think labelers are so important that I keep an extra one in my car. I never know when or where I will be when I need to label something. As they say in the American Express motto, "Don't leave home without it!"

Labels are a crucial part of organization. A clear plastic container without a label is like a cake without icing. Labels add so much! They give a clean, organized look, and even when a container is clear, reading a label is easier and faster than peering through the container to see what's inside.

After you fill a container, label it on all four sides. That way, if the container gets pulled out and replaced backwards, a label is still visible. Once you begin labeling, I guarantee that you will not be able to stop!

MEASURE FIRST, SHOP SECOND

Don't forget to take measurements of your space before going shopping for organizing tools. Measure the height, width, and depth of the space you are organizing. Jot down the measurements and take them with you. Few things are more frustrating than returning from the store to discover that your purchased items are either too small or too large. You'll avoid these mishaps if you take the time to do this preliminary work.

Many organizing tools have measurements written on the packaging. However, I recommend bringing a tape measure to the store with you, just in case. This way you can actually measure the products you're considering buying, if necessary.

Shopping for organizing products is fun, but it can also be frustrating. Most likely you will not find everything you need under one roof. The two stores that are closest to one-stop-shopping are The Container Store and Organized Living. Other stores to descend upon are Bed Bath & Beyond, Linens-n-Things, Kmart, Target, and Wal-Mart. Don't forget to bring your shopping list to the store with you. Bring this book along with you, too. It will be a good reference guide. Use the pictures to lead you to the right tools.

PICK YOUR PROJECTS

You'll find dozens of organizing "recipes" in this book. Each recipe includes an estimated amount of time each area may take you to organize. This is an approximation, not a definite amount of time. The time will fluctuate between individuals, depending on the size of the room or task, the amount of clutter, and personal abilities. Use the timelines as guides to help direct you, to keep you focused, and to help keep up a good work pace.

For each organizing "recipe," I've also indicated the level of difficulty: easy, moderate, difficult, and combinations of those. Your skill level will determine if certain tasks are easier or more difficult for you than others. I based these levels on my experience working alongside hundreds of homeowners. Read the directions for each task thoroughly before beginning, keeping in mind the level of difficulty. Consider which tasks you will take on alone and which ones you may require assistance to complete.

Once you've found a project that fits the amount of time you have and your skill level, it's time to dig in!

Each organizing "recipe" also includes a list of the organizing tools that you will need to complete the project. Each recipe is then broken down into steps, many of which are illustrated to help guide you as you work to complete the task.

PART TWO

Clothes and Closets

A WELL-ORGANIZED DRAWER MAKES IT EASY TO SEE
THE CONTENTS AT A GLANCE. FINDING WHAT YOU
NEED TAKES MERE SECONDS!

Chapter 4

Drawers, Drawers, and More Drawers

Kitchen drawers, desk drawers, bathroom drawers, nightstand drawers, chests of drawers, stacking drawers—there are many kinds of drawers! But here's a secret: All drawers require the same process if anything other than clothing is placed inside. We'll get to clothing in the next chapter, but I wanted to ease you into a quick and rewarding project to start off. So pick a drawer and let's go!

Beverly Hills Top Tip

If the drawer organizers slide or move about when opening and closing the drawer, remove the drawer organizers, attach Velcro to the bottoms and place them back inside the drawer.

BASIC DRAWER ORGANIZATION

TOTAL TIME
30–45 minutes (per drawer)

DEGREE OF DIFFICULTY
Easy

TOOLS
drawer organizers and tension dividers

1. Measure the inside of the drawer that needs organizing. Take the measurements with you to the store when making tool purchases.

2. Purchase drawer organizers and tension dividers to accommodate the size of the drawer.

3. Place the drawer organizers on a counter or desk located on top of the drawer that is being organized.

4. Remove the items from the drawer and sort them into piles of like items. For example, put all of the pencils together in one pile and all of the pens, rubber bands, paper clips, and markers in other piles. If you have any papers in the drawer, gather them up and set them aside. We'll talk about dealing with paperwork and home offices in detail in chapter 13.

5. For each item category, select a space within the drawer organizer that is big enough to hold the items. For example, if this is the designated drawer for scissors, make sure all of the scissors will fit into the space in which you intend to put them. This process is very much like a puzzle. Do not get frustrated—have fun! This is the creative part of the job. Place the items inside the drawer organizers.

6. Discard everything that is no longer needed or wanted. This is a great time to spring clean!

7. Wipe the inside of the drawer clean with your favorite cleaning product.

8. Place the filled drawer organizer inside the drawer.

9. Continue this process with every drawer in your home and office.

Note: Tension dividers are spring-loaded partitions that divide a drawer into sections. These dividers can be used in conjunction with drawer organizers or on their own.

Beverly Hills Top Tip

It's a key organizing principle that you will create more space when you place items upright inside a drawer, instead of stacked on top of each other. Plus, you'll be able to see everything from a bird's-eye view. So don't stack things unless you have multiples of the same items, such as paper-clip boxes, staples, and Post-it Notes.

I LOVE THIS SIMPLE BIN SYSTEM FOR STORING TONS
OF CLOTHES IN A SMALL SPACE.

Chapter 5

Folding and Hanging Clothes

Storing clothing can be a major organizing challenge. Simply put, there are two ways to store clothing: You can fold it, or you can hang it. We'll cover each of these in turn.

FOLDING CLOTHES

Folding is a technique that, if done properly, will provide you with extra drawer space, a bird's-eye view of all the contents inside the drawer (no more searching!), and aesthetic pleasure and pride.

Folded clothing should only be placed in drawers in one direction—upright. Don't stack things on top of each other in piles. I know this may surprise you, but think about it: Keeping clothes in piles inside of drawers forces you to dig, like a cat in a litter box.

Think about all the clothing you have in drawers right now. I'll bet you have not worn 50 percent of those items, because you either could not see them or you forgot about them altogether. When clothing is placed upright in a drawer, you can see everything at once. This is what I call the bird's-eye view.

When you can't store folded clothing upright is when it's being stored, not in a drawer, but on a shelf. To keep stacks of garments neat and orderly,

See how many tops will go in a single drawer when they're placed upright? And you can see every one of them!

especially when you need to pull out things that are not on the top of the pile, use an organizing tool called Fold 'n Stax, thin sheets of plastic that go between each folded garment. Fold 'n Stax sheets make it possible to remove a garment easily without disturbing the remaining pieces, keeping all other folded items perfectly organized.

Another way to keep folded clothing organized on a shelf is to store it upright in baskets.

In this section, we'll talk about folding T-shirts, tank tops, shorts, socks, and underwear, the items that people generally store in dresser drawers. Before you begin to fold, determine in which drawers the folded garments will be placed. This is important because the secret to folding things well is to fold them to fit the size of the drawer. The folded items are literally fitted to the space in which they will be placed. For example, if a drawer is 24 inches wide, fold each T-shirt to 8 inches wide, making three vertical rows.

Occasionally, a drawer will not accommodate our clothes so perfectly. You may have space to make three vertical rows front to back and have a small area left on one side. Utilize the remaining space by putting garments in to fill that area.

The key to having beautiful sock, bra, and underpants drawers is to use organizing tools called sock, bra, and brief boxes. These boxes come in lots of different materials, such as clear plastic, leather, and wood. By using these tools, you will have the picture-perfect drawer that you thought was only possible in a magazine. These systems are extremely easy to maintain, and they're worth every minute spent putting them in order.

FOLDING LONG-SLEEVED T-SHIRTS

 TOTAL TIME:
less than 2 minutes (per shirt)

●● **DEGREE OF DIFFICULTY:**
easy to moderate (depending on your patience and skill level)

人 **TOOLS:**
none required

1. Place the T-shirt face down on a table.

2. Begin the fold at the edge of the neckline. Fold the left side of the T-shirt over one-third. Smooth out the fabric with your hand.

3. Fold the left sleeve of the T-shirt back and down, and smooth out the fabric.

4. Fold the right side of the T-shirt over one-third, covering the left fold. Smooth out the fabric with your hand.

5. Fold the right sleeve back and down, and smooth out the fabric.

6. Begin to fold the T-shirt, from bottom to top.

7. Measure the depth of the drawer. Depending on the depth, either fold the T-shirt in half again or fold it into thirds. The goal is for the folded T-shirt to stand upright in the drawer.

8. Check that the T-shirts will stand up on end upright in the drawer.

9. Color-coordinate the T-shirts and place them upright inside the drawer.

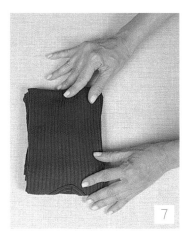

FOLDING SHIRTS WITH SPAGHETTI STRAPS AND TANK TOPS

 TOTAL TIME:
less than 2 minutes (per shirt)

● **DEGREE OF DIFFICULTY:**
easy

 **TOOLS:**
none required

1. Place the top face-down on a table.

2. Fold down the straps to the armpit area.

3. Fold the left side of the top over one-third.

4. Fold the right side of the top over one-third, covering the left side.

5. Measure the depth of the drawer. Depending on the depth, either fold the top in half and in half again or fold it into thirds. The goal is for the folded top to fit upright in the drawer.

6. Check that the top will stand up on end upright in the drawer.

7. Color-coordinate the tops and place them upright inside the drawer.

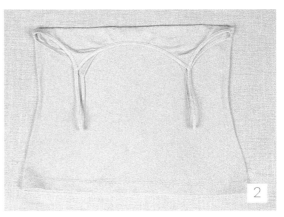

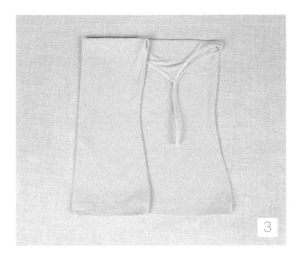

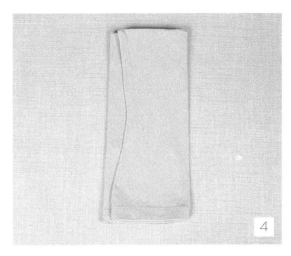

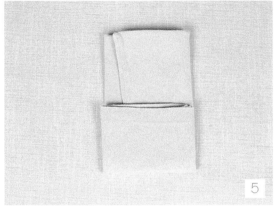

Folding Lightweight Gym Shorts

⏱ **TOTAL TIME:**
less than 2 minutes (per pair of shorts)

● **DEGREE OF DIFFICULTY:**
easy

🪝 **TOOLS:**
none required

1. Hold the shorts sideways, lining up the two legs.

2. Lay the shorts down on a table.

3. Fold the shorts from the length into thirds (for larger sizes) or in half (for smaller sizes).

4. Fold the shorts from the bottom to the waist in half and in half again, or in thirds (depending on the depth of the drawer).

5. Color-coordinate the shorts and place them upright inside the drawer.

Note: Follow these directions for folding boxer shorts. Place the folded boxer shorts inside a brief box.

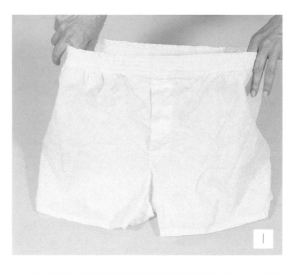

3

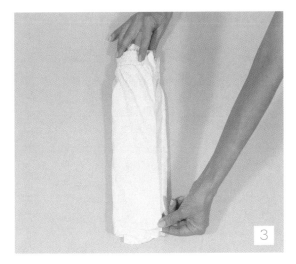

3

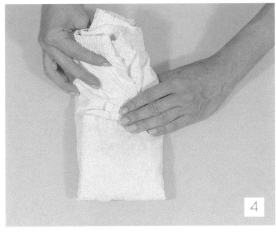

4

4

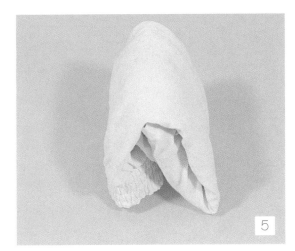

5

FOLDING BULKIER SHORTS

 TOTAL TIME:
less than 2 minutes (per pair of shorts)

● **DEGREE OF DIFFICULTY:**
easy

TOOLS:
none required

1. Hold the shorts sideways, lining up the two legs.

2. Fold the shorts from the length, in half or thirds, depending on the depth of the drawer.

3. Place the shorts inside the drawer horizontally with the rounded edge facing up.

FOLDING SOCKS

Save the life of your socks and create more space in your drawer by purchasing sock boxes. Folding and turning your socks inside out in a ball does two bad things: It creates bulk in the drawer, and it deteriorates the elastic in the socks more rapidly. If you're rolling your socks now, try my method and see how much better it is!

 TOTAL TIME:
less than 1 minute (per pair of socks)

● **DEGREE OF DIFFICULTY:**
easy

TOOLS:
sock boxes

1. Take a pair of socks and line them up, one on top of the other.

2. Fold the pair of socks in half.

3. Fold the pair of socks in half again.

4. Place the pair of folded socks inside the sock box, color-coordinated, with the rounded edges facing up.

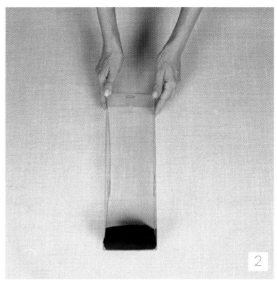

FOLDING THONGS

Underpants shouldn't be stacked on top of each other inside of drawers, either. They too need to folded and stored upright. My dear friend, Niecy Nash, has been known to say that I fold underwear into origamis. She's not that far off with her description. Underwear requires folding; make it pretty at the same time!

 TOTAL TIME:
less than 1 minute (per thong)

● **DEGREE OF DIFFICULTY:**
easy

TOOLS:
sock box

1. Place a thong, front side down, on a table

2. Fold the crotch portion of the thong up to meet the waistband.

3. Fold each side over the crotch in a crisscross fashion.

4. Place the thong upright inside a sock box with the rounded edge facing up.

5. Color-coordinate the thongs if desired.

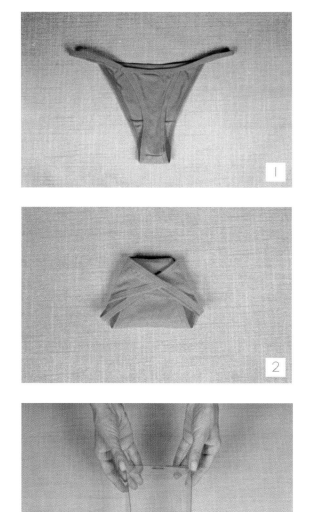

FOLDING UNDERPANTS AND BRIEFS

 TOTAL TIME:
less than 1 minute
(per pair of underpants)

● **DEGREE OF DIFFICULTY:**
easy

TOOLS:
sock or brief boxes

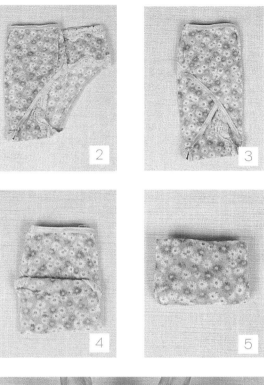

1. Place a pair of underpants on a table, back-side down.

2. Fold over the left side, one-third.

3. Fold over the right side, one-third, covering the left side fold.

4. Fold the crotch up one-third.

5. Fold the crotch up again, in half.

6. With the rounded edge facing up, place the underpants inside a sock or brief box, depending on the size of the underwear.

7. Color-coordinate the underpants if desired.

FOLDING BRAS

 TOTAL TIME:
less than 1 minute (per bra)

● **DEGREE OF DIFFICULTY:**
easy

TOOLS:
bra box

1. Place a bra on a table, face down.

2. Fold the left side of the bra over the right side, lining up the cups.

3. Pick up the bra in your hands. Smooth the cups and straps out evenly.

4. Fold the back of the bra over into the inside of the cup. Fold back and zigzag any remaining portions, hiding the entire back of the bra inside the cups.

5. Fold the straps down into the cups of the bra.

6. Place the bra upright inside a bra box.

7. Color-coordinate the bras, if desired.

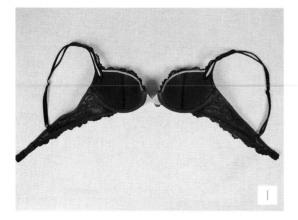

FOLDING TOWELS

The key to folding towels is to fold them to fit the space in which they will be stored. Make sure the rounded edges face out. The linen closet or open shelving where you store your towels can look like the ones in department stores with very little effort. Then it will be time to stand back and admire your towels! No more shoving them in and trying to slam the door closed. The folding technique presented here is for all sizes of towels.

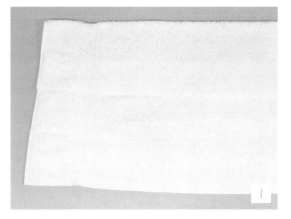

 TOTAL TIME:
less than 2 minutes (per towel)

● **DEGREE OF DIFFICULTY:**
easy

TOOLS:
none required

1. Determine where the towels will be stored.

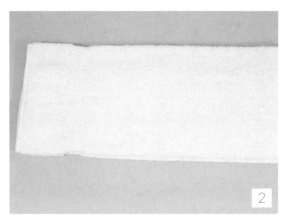

2. Measure the length and width of that area. If necessary, cut a piece of butcher paper or newspaper the size of the shelf, to use as your template to fold on. Remember, you are folding to fit the space.

3. In linen closets in which there is deep space, fold the entire length of the shelf. You want long flat stacks of towels, utilizing the entire space of the shelf. The goal: No more piles in front of piles. Unless you have enough of the same type of towel to create one stack in front of the other, fold the towels so that they fill the entire depth of the shelves.

4. Lay a towel down on top of a table, counter, or bed.

5. Fold the length of the towel into thirds by taking the left side and folding it one-third and then folding the right side over the left side, one-third.

Continued on next page

6. You now have two options, depending on depth of your shelf space. Option #1: Fold the towel in half so that the two bottom edges meet. You may also need to fold it in half again. Option #2: Fold the towel from the bottom up, one third and fold the top down, one third. Check to see which size best fits your shelf.

Note: Option #2 may not create exact "thirds" to fit your space. Work with it until the entire shelf is covered from front to back. Beach towels or large bath towels may work best using this option.

7. Keep the first towel you fold as a guide to fold the remaining towels. This way, all of the towels will be uniformly folded.

8. Place the towels on the shelf, with their rounded edges facing out.

9. Color-coordinate the towels, if desired.

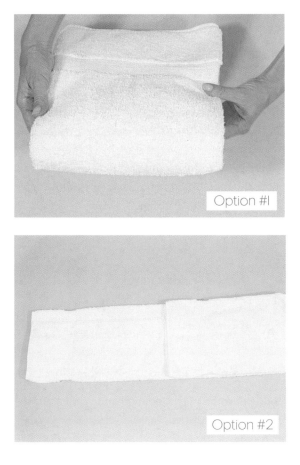

Option #1

Option #2

Beverly Hills Top Tip

Here's another option for storing towels: You can roll them up and place them upright inside a basket next to the bathtub.

FOLDING FLAT SHEETS

Bed linens can be a folding challenge, especially fitted sheets. Fold the flat sheets and pillowcases the same way they come in packages. The keys are to keep them uniform in size and to always place the rounded edges facing out.

It is a matter of your personal preference whether you prefer to store the sheets together as a set or store the pillowcases separately.

 TOTAL TIME:
about 3 minutes
(per sheet, depending on the size of the sheet)

● **DEGREE OF DIFFICULTY:**
easy

 TOOLS:
none required

1. Fold the sheet in half, from the bottom of the sheet to the top.

2. Fold the sheet in half again.

3. Fold the sheet from the width, in half and in half again. The sheet is now a square with one rounded edge.

4. Fold the sheet in from the two sides (not the side with the rounded edge) into thirds, keeping the edges from the second fold back about 1 inch from being seen on the outer edge. The sheet will resemble a jelly roll, with two smooth edges and two open ends.

5. Starting from one open end, fold the sheet into thirds.

6. Place the folded sheet on the shelf, with the rounded edge facing out.

Beverly Hills Top Tip

Ironed sheets are always easier to fold.

FOLDING FITTED SHEETS

TOTAL TIME:
3 to 5 minutes (per sheet, depending on the size
of the sheet—more patience required here!)

● **DEGREE OF DIFFICULTY:**
easy

 TOOLS:
none required

1. Begin the fold from the bottom of the sheet to
the top.

2. Line up the fitted corners.

3. Tuck the two corners inside each other, creating a rectangular shape with the sheet.

4. Fold the sheet in half again.

5. Fold the sheet from the width, in half and in
half again. The sheet is now a square with one
rounded edge.

6. Fold the sheet in from the two sides (not the side
with the rounded edge) into thirds, keeping the
edges from the second fold back about 1 inch
from being seen on the outer edge. The sheet
will resemble a jelly roll, with two smooth edges
and two open ends.

7. Starting from one open end, fold the sheet into
thirds.

8. Place the folded sheet on the shelf, with the
rounded edge facing out.

FOLDING PILLOWCASES

TOTAL TIME:
less than 1 minute (per pillowcase)

● **DEGREE OF DIFFICULTY:**
easy

TOOLS:
none required

1. Starting from the open end, fold the pillowcase
in half and in half again. It will resemble a
jelly roll, with two smooth edges and two open
ends.

2. Starting from one open end, fold the pillowcase into thirds.

3. Place the pillowcase on the shelf, with the
rounded edge facing out.

HANGING CLOTHES

My all-time favorite line from a movie is, "No more wire hangers, ever!" This quote was from the movie *Mommie Dearest*, the Joan Crawford story. Simply put, wire hangers do not look good. A big part of organization is the final look of the space. No closet will ever be complete without some type of attractive hangers, such as white plastic tubular hangers, padded hangers, or wooden hangers. Wire hangers do not fit the category.

Choose a hanger you like and stick with it. A uniform look is more attractive than a cluster of mixed hangers. I prefer white tubular hangers because they are inexpensive, durable, and have a clean appearance.

HANGING CLOTHING

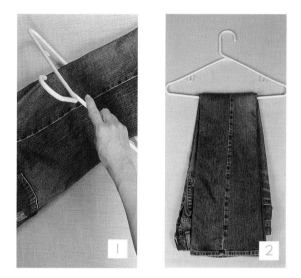

 TOTAL TIME:
less than 30 seconds (per piece of clothing)

● **DEGREE OF DIFFICULTY:**
easy

TOOLS:
type of hangers of your choice for shirts, pants, and skirts

1. Decide which way all of the clothing in your closet should face. Consider how you enter your closet. If the closet is a reach-in and the door is on the right, you will hang the clothes differently than if the door was on the left side. Hang your clothing so that the front of the clothing faces you as you navigate through your wardrobe.

2. Hang all of the clothing on the hangers in the same direction. Think of a department store and how the clothing is hanging on the rods. It is always hung with the front of the clothes facing the same direction. Place all of the clothing on the hangers and in the closet.

Note: There are two options for hanging slacks: You can hang them long on pants hangers or you can hang them folded at the knee over the hanger. To fold slacks over the hanger, take the front opening and fold it so that the two legs line up sideways, forming a crease down the center of the legs. Put the legs through the hanger with the backside of the slacks facing out toward you.

A WELL-DESIGNED AND ORGANIZED CLOSET IS A JOY
TO BEHOLD—AND THE SECRET TO CONTROLLING
CLUTTER THROUGHOUT THE HOUSE.

Chapter 6

Closets

Well-organized closets are the secret behind clutter-free rooms. On *Clean House*, the Style Network show I co-host, the designers cannot do their magic without a clean palette. It's up to me to find a place to hide the necessities and unmentionables in an accessible fashion.

There are three ways to take on the task of creating great closets: You can have them custom-built, use a handyman, or do it yourself. All three require designing the space to accommodate the contents.

Custom-built closets are the most expensive. Relying solely on a closet designer from the company of your choice can be a big mistake. Many points must be considered and factored into the design. It is not uncommon to spend a large sum of money on custom closets and be disappointed with the final product. Generally, you will not be aware that the design is flawed until you are putting your things away.

To avoid costly mistakes on any of the three ways—custom, handyman, and do-it-yourself closets—you must do your homework first. That's why I'm here to help with Closet Design 101.

CLOSET DESIGN 101

Before we get to the specific projects, I'd like to take you through the closet design process. Designing closets is a mathematical exercise. You'll need to do a few simple math equations to get the proportions right. (Don't worry—I'll help you.) Here's how it works.

1. First, learn how to read a tape measure. You'll be using it in a minute.

2. Sort the clothing in your closet by keeping all like items together. Place all of the shirts together, all of the pants together, etc.

3. Measure the linear footage (the amount of hanging space from left to right you need to hang your clothes) that is taken up in the closet by groups: shirts and blouses, long-hanging pants, pants that are hanging folded at the knees, long dresses, short dresses, suits, and skirts. Write down your findings. For example:

Shirts = 24"-wide space
Skirts = 18"-wide space
Pants = 34"-wide space

4. Count the number of shoes and add the shoe count to the linear list. A pair of standard women's shoes is 8" wide, and a pair of men's shoes is 9" wide. Given this information, in order to get three pairs of women's shoes, side by side, on one shelf, the inside dimensions of the shelf must be 24" (8" x 3 pairs), and three pairs of men's shoes side by side need 27 inches (9" x 3 pairs). If these measurements are not part of the equation, your closet can be "off."

5. Measure the length of each type of clothing, from the closet rod to the bottom of the garment. Here are rule-of-thumb measurements for a person of average height:

TYPE OF CLOTHING	WOMEN	MEN
Shirts	32"–36"	36"–42"
Long pants	48"–56"	56" +
Pants folded	34"–36"	36" +
Short dresses	56"	
Long dresses	65"	
Long skirts	56"	

Now consider how much height space you'll need for shoes. There are two ways to use shelves for shoes: straight or tilted. Generally, shoe shelves are spaced 6" apart. Straight shelves allow also for adjusting shelf space up or down.

Tilted shelves are 8" apart, and they are not adjustable (unless wire shelving is used). Tilted shelves also require installation of a "toe kick" or "fence," to keep the shoes from sliding off the shelf. (Wire shelving can be turned upside down to

Also measure the width of partitions; they also take up space. Generally, most partitions are between $1/2$" to $3/4$" inches wide. If a closet has four partitions that are $3/4$" inches wide each, 3" will be lost in the linear footage of the closet.

The partitions in your closet shouldn't be more than 30" apart. This is due to the weight of the clothing. If the width is too great between partitions, the rod will bow and could eventually break free of the partition. This is especially true for men's clothing, which is heavier than women's clothing.

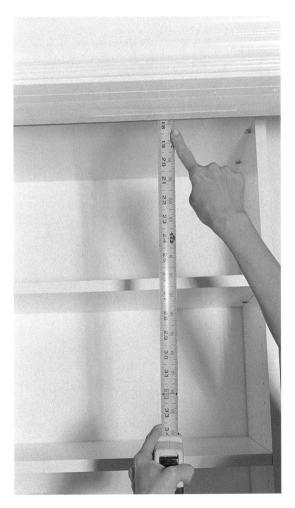

create a shoe fence. (You'll find other shoe options in the Do-It-Yourself section on page 62.)

6. Measure the interior of the closet: ceiling height, width, depth, and soffit. (The soffit is the space from above the opening of the closet door to the ceiling. This is an important measurement, because if the top shelf is too high, it will not be accessible due to the soffit.)

7. Using graph paper, plot the measurements of your closet to scale to get an overview.

8. Measure any partitions in the closet and add them to the graph of the closet. (Partitions are the vertical wall panels between which closet rods are attached.)

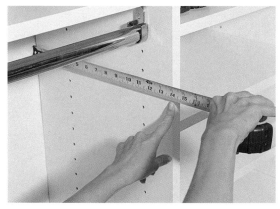

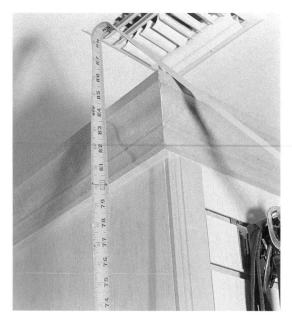

Most partitions are 14" deep, and when clothing is hanging on the rod, it extends into the space up to 22" deep.

Skirts and pants stay within the 14" partitions, but shirts and dresses don't. The reason these figures are so important is because they will determine your movement in the closet and the accessibility of clothes and shoes in the closet.

9. Consider if you want your closet to have drawers. Standard drawer widths are 18" and 24". My preference is 24" wide. This is not to say that you can't order custom sizes. However, there is always an added fee for custom sizes. Another option is to purchase a small tower of drawers. Either way, if you are considering putting drawers in the closet, don't forget to plot them on your overview, too.

10. Once you are satisfied with the layout of the overview, it is time to prepare the elevations

Elevations are the plans used to build the closet. (See page 61 for examples from a closet I designed.) An elevation has to be prepared for each wall on which something will be built. Even if you don't go this far because you are working with a custom closet company, at least you will have an excellent idea of how your space will best function. Refer to the elevation example on page 61 and draw your own.

There are other little things you need to be aware of. In a walk-in closet, there is always some dead space in the corners. Not every inch is useable space. You must have reach-in space. There are two solutions for designing around the dead corner space: You can allow 18" of space at corners or at the adjoining side walls by connecting the corners.

Closets 101: Before and After

Here's how Closet Design 101 works in real life. One of my clients had decided to convert her guest bedroom into a walk-in closet. But the idea of a "walk-in" ended at the threshold. Her dream of space and order had ended in a jungle of impenetrable piles and haphazard, overstuffed hanging items. There were even three-basket systems buried in the middle of the room!

But I wasn't daunted. I used the simple shelving system called ShelfTrack by ClosetMaid, and I repurposed the homeowner's cube wall. I also repurposed the basket systems for T-shirts, scarves, and undergarments.

Before: This room has the potential to become a spacious closet. But what a mess! It looks more like the back room of a second-hand store.

After: Using my Closet Design 101 guidelines, I transformed the messy closet into this attractive, hardworking space. It's hard to believe that it's the same room!

Here's my master plan of the closet, along with two elevation drawings I made so I could plot how to place the design elements.

I designed this walk-in closet following my directions for Closet Design 101. I first made an overview of the entire space. Then I counted the shoes and measured the clothing. This homeowner had 13 linear feet of 36"-length clothing (double-hung = 6½ feet), 7 linear feet of medium-length clothing, 52" in length, and 200 pairs of shoes! (See the overview and elevations at right see how I used these measurements in my design.) Knowing the exact amount of clothes and shoes you need to accommodate is imperative in order to design a closet that will fit your needs.

This closet took approximately twenty hours to empty, install ShelfTrack, and return the clothing to its proper place. I created this true walk-in closet for less than $350!

So that's how the system works. Now let's start on some projects.

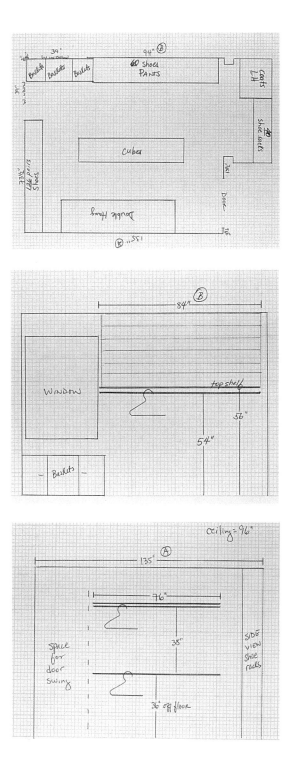

CREATING A DO-IT-YOURSELF BEDROOM CLOSET

Your closet is one of the most frequently visited places in your home. This area should be in top form. When the closet space works without a snag, your day starts off on the right foot. Imagine having a place for all of your clothing, neatly organized and color-coordinated. Digging and searching *can* be things of the past!

 TOTAL TIME:
6 to 8 hours

● **DEGREE OF DIFFICULTY:**
easy

TOOLS:
double hangs, shower rod cover, medium stacking shelves, long stacking shelves, white tubular hangers or hangers of your choice (no wire hangers!), skirt hangers, HangaDanga portable hanger organizer, shoe rack, and boot shapers

OPTIONAL TOOLS:
drawer chest, sock boxes, hanging organizers, belt rack or belt hanger, mirror valet, and storage keepers

1. First, measure the distance from the rod to the floor. If the measurement is less than 72" (6 feet), the rod will need to be raised to 72". This may require a handyman's services. It is a simple procedure, and it *must* be done. If a rod is less than 72" off the floor, you will lose valuable storage space. In order to double hang, meaning doubling your existing rod space, the rod has to be 72" in height to keep clothes from dragging on the floor of the closet.

2. Empty the closet into piles of like items. If you have clothing that has not been worn in two years or that you have been saving because it was expensive, or you are waiting to lose weight, ask yourself these questions: Does it still feel good to wear? Is it still in fashion? If the answer to either question is no, donate it to charity. (See page 25 for information about charities.)

3. Raise the rod and the shelf above the rod if necessary.

4. Refer to Closet Design 101, Steps 3, 4, and 5 on pages 55 and 56. Purchase the tools that will accommodate your clothing. For example, you may need two double hangs. It is extremely important to do your preliminary homework before making purchases. Few things are more frustrating than having to make another store run when you are in the throes of organizing.

5. Put the shower rod cover on the rod. The cover serves two purposes: The hangers will move smoothly on the rod, and the rod cover gives the appearance that the closet has recently been painted, a very fresh look.

6. Place the double hang on the rod. (See page 69 for an example of a beautiful child's closet with a double hang in place.)

7. Use the medium and long stacking shelves to customize the top shelf in the closet. Measure the space between the shelf and the ceiling. Measure the length of the shelf. The height and width of the space will determine how many stacking shelves are required to customize this area.

8. Install the optional tools. A drawer chest can be used in addition to a dresser, or it can eliminate a dresser completely from the room, bringing all your clothing inside the closet to open up the bedroom. Sock boxes keep drawers organized. Hanging organizers are useful for purses, sweaters, and sweatshirts. If needed, install a belt rack or belt hanger.

9. Transfer the clothing to the tubular and skirt hangers. Place each piece of clothing on the hangers in the same direction. Store leftover tubular hangers on a HangaDanga portable hanger organizer.

10. Return the clothing to the closet. Because the clothing is already in piles of like items, return it to the closet this way: blouses and shirts by sleeve length (sleeveless to long-sleeve) and light colors to dark colors, pants and slacks from light colors to dark colors, and dresses and skirts from the shortest to longest and by color.

11. Install the shoe rack. Place the shoe rack against one of the side walls (not the back wall) of the closet. If you install it on the back wall, it will take up too much precious storage space.

12. Place shoes on the shoe rack from most frequently used on the outer portion of the rack to least worn towards the back of the closet wall.

13. Use boot shapers to keep tall boots from flopping over and to keep their shape. Boots can also be stored lying down on a top shelf, taking up less vertical space.

14. If you'd like, hang a mirror valet on the inside of the closet door, giving you nearly a full-body reflection. Open the valet for space to keep ties, belts, jewelry, and more.

15. If you'd like, store items you want to protect from insects and bugs inside storage keepers. There is a variety of storage keepers available, including those for sweaters, hanging garments, comforters, and blankets.

16. Fill the closet with the remaining garments and storage.

THE HANDYMAN CLOSET

If you don't want to do the construction work on your closet but don't want to pay a specialty closet company to install an expensive custom-closet either, using the skills of a handyman is a good option. The catch is that you still need to design the closet yourself.

When you're designing a closet for a handyman to install, you'll need to use the steps you learned in Closet Design 101. You can create a closet that has a custom look without the high cost, if you follow those steps. (Refer to the sample elevation on page 61 to refresh your memory about how to draw elevations for your handyman closet.)

The difference between a custom and handyman closet is that in a handyman closet, the rods are not adjustable. This means that the measurements must be accurate when you're designing the elevations. If they are incorrect, for example, the clothing that is double hung may not have enough space between rods, or it may drag on the floor.

When a Handyman Really Comes in Handy

A good handyman is worth his (or her) weight in gold. I use a handyman every time I need to build a non-custom closet. Handymen can generally build you anything, but it is up to you to provide them with a plan. Designing a closet a handyman can install will take some planning. Even though you are technically building a custom closet, I differentiate a handyman closet from a custom closet, since it is not being built by a closet company and the cost is substantially less.

Beverly Hills Top Tip

If space permits, you can add storage space to your closet with adjustable shelving by simply using inexpensive bookcases. Purchase additional shelves to create shoe shelves. (Here's a rule of thumb: Place shoe shelves approximately 6" apart.)

Remember that a pair of women's shoes is 8" wide, and a pair of men's shoes is 9" wide. Figure out the number of additional shelves needed by taking a shoe count. For example: If your shelves are 24" wide and you have 15 pairs of shoes at 3 pairs of women's shoes fit per shelf, you'll need 5 shelves. In the same scenario with men's shoes, you'll be able to fit two and a half pairs per shelf, and you'll need 6 shelves. To fit more shoes across, stagger them, by keeping pairs together but placing one shoe slightly in front of the other.

Secure each bookcase by anchoring it to the wall. This technique, using store-bought bookcases, gives the closet a custom look. You will be amazed!

Design the closet in individual sections to accommodate your wardrobe. The handyman will custom-build each section following those specifications. Each section needs to have measurements for the width, number of shelves, and number of feet and inches it needs to be off the floor. When the closet is filled with clothing, it will appear nearly as gorgeous as a custom-built closet and have all the functionality.

You can also get beautiful results with ClosetMaid closet kits or by purchasing ClosetMaid products individually. ClosetMaid's wire shelf track systems or MasterSuites Collection can be installed by a handyman quickly and easily, giving a custom-closet look without the high cost.

DESIGNING A HANDYMAN CLOSET

 TOTAL TIME:
10 to 16 hours
(depending on the size of the closet)

●●● **DEGREE OF DIFFICULTY:**
moderate to difficult

TOOLS:
depending on your closet, may include medium-density fiber board, 2 ½" drywall screws, 1 ¼" drywall screws, 2" by 3" pine boards for supports, closet rods, primer, paint, and white melamine bookcases and extra shelves or ClosetMaid closet kits or wire shelving, shower rod cover, white tubular hangers or hangers of your choice (no wire hangers!), skirts hangers, HangaDanga portable hanger organizer, medium stacking shelves, and long stacking shelves

OPTIONAL TOOLS:
shoe rack, drawer chest, sock boxes, hanging organizer, and belt hanger or belt rack

1. Empty the closet into piles of like items. If you have clothing that has not been worn in two years or that you have been saving because it was expensive or you are waiting to lose weight, ask yourself these questions: Does it still feel good to wear? Is it still in fashion? If the answer to either question is no, donate it to charity. (See the Beverly Hills Top Tip on page 000 about charities.)

2. Supply the handyman with the overview and elevations for the closet. (See "Closet Design 101" on page 53 for instructions on how to create the overview and elevations.) Purchase the equipment to build the closet. The equipment will depend on your particular situation, but it's like to include medium-density fiber board, 2 ½" drywall screws, 1¼" drywall screws, 2" by 3" inch pine boards for supports, closet rods,

> ### *Beverly Hills Top Tip*
>
> Use Neat 'n Ups shelf liner on wire shelving that will be used for smaller items, to prevent items from slipping through the wire shelves. Neat 'n Ups are particularly useful on wire shoe shelving, to prevent heels from slipping through the wire shelves. They also make dusting a breeze.

primer, paint, and white melamine bookcases and extra shelves or ClosetMaid closet kits or wire shelving. Let the construction begin!

3. When the construction is complete, put the shower rod cover on the rod. The cover serves two purposes: The hangers move smoothly on the rod, and the shower rod cover gives the appearance that the closet has recently been painted, a very fresh look.

4. Transfer the clothing over to the tubular and skirt hangers. Place all of the clothing on the hangers in the same direction. Store leftover tubular hangers on a HangaDanga portable hanger organizer.

5. Return the clothing to the closet. Since the clothing is already in piles of like items, return it to the closet this way: blouses and shirts by sleeve length (sleeveless to long-sleeve) and light colors to dark colors, pants and slacks from light colors to dark colors, and dresses and skirts from the shortest to longest and by color.

6. If your closet has a shoe rack, place it against one of the side walls (not the back wall) of the closet. If you install it on the back wall, it will take up too much precious storage space. (See page 63 for a photo of a shoe rack in place.)

7. Return the shoes to the bookcase/shoe shelves or shoe rack. Place shoes on the shoe rack from most frequently used on the outer portion of the rack to least worn towards the back of the closet wall.

8. If your closet has a drawer chest, which can eliminate a dresser from the bedroom, freeing up space, add sock boxes to keep drawers organized and save valuable space. (See "Folding Socks" on page 43 for more on sock boxes.)

9. Use the medium and long stacking shelves to customize the top shelf in the closet. Measure the space between the shelf and the ceiling. Measure the length of the shelf. The height and width of the space will determine how many stacking shelves are required to customize this area.

10. If you're using a hanging organizer and belt hanger or belt rack, install them.

11. Fill the closet with the remaining garments and storage.

CHILDREN'S CLOSETS

My credo is that organization should be easy, obtainable, maintainable, and begun at an early age. The gift of organization is one of the greatest gifts you can give your children. Organization is a lifestyle, and begun early, it will have an enormously positive impact on your children's lives— how they view their surroundings, how they treat their belongings and others' belongings, how they conduct themselves, and how they develop their schoolwork habits. Organization spills over into every aspect of our lives.

A well-organized child's closet provides a foundation on which your child can build his or her skills, promote and develop responsibility, and take pride in his or her space.

The idea behind designing children's closets is that the closets will grow as the children's needs change and as the children grow. For the closet to grow, it must be adjustable. An inexpensive way to accomplish this goal is by using ClosetMaid products. ClosetMaid is made for do-it-yourself installation. The products are available in both melamine and polyurethane-coated wire and can be purchased from retail stores.

ORGANIZING A CHILD'S CLOSET

⏱ **TOTAL TIME:**
8 to 10 hours
(depending on the choice of closet materials)

●● **DEGREE OF DIFFICULTY:**
moderate

⚲ **TOOLS:**
ClosetMaid closet kit, Neat 'n Ups shelf liners, clear plastic containers to hold toys, child-size tubular hangers, skirt hangers (if needed), shoe rack, and hooks

A child's closet can become part of the room if you remove the closet doors.

1. Review Closet Design 101 on page 53. Often, children have more toys than clothes. Figure toys into the design element. Shelving designed for toys can be converted later into shelving for sweaters, sweatshirts, and shoes. The goal is to have a clutter-free room.

2. Empty the closet, sorting the items into piles of like items.

3. Gut the closet by removing all existing rods and shelves.

4. Measure your closet (per Closet Design 101 on page 53) and choose the ClosetMaid kit that fits your needs. Follow the directions provided with the closet installation kit.

5. Place Neat 'n Ups shelf liners on wire shelving that will be used for smaller items, to prevent items from slipping through the wire shelves.

6. Store toys inside clear plastic containers and label the outside. Labeling promotes reading for younger children. Labeling also gives a clean, neat, organized look. Using clear containers allows you to see what's inside the containers without opening them, unlike opaque containers. Don't transfer toys to different-sized containers; instead, create piles of "like toy items" before choosing the container, so they will all fit on the first attempt.

7. Place the filled toy containers on the shelves.

8. Transfer the clothing to the child-size tubular and skirt hangers. Place all of the clothing on the hangers in the same direction.

9. Return the clothing to the closet. Since the clothing is already in piles of like items, return it to the closet this way: shirts by sleeve length (sleeveless to long-sleeve) and light colors to dark colors, pants from light colors to dark colors, and dresses and skirts from the shortest to longest and by color.

10. Organize shoes. Individual, stackable shoe racks are perfect for children's closets. Each rack holds three pairs of shoes and is stackable. Purchase the number of racks you need to accommodate the number of shoes your child has. For example, if a child has five pairs of shoes, purchase two racks. Place the shoe rack against one of the side walls (not the back wall) of the closet. If you install it straight on, it will take up too much precious storage space.

11. Place the shoes on the shoe rack from most frequently used on the outer portion of the rack to least worn towards the back of the closet wall.

12. Install hooks on the walls inside the closet for purses, belts, and other hanging items.

13. Fill the closet with the remaining garments and storage.

LINEN CLOSETS

There are two common problems with linen closets: They're often too deep, and there's frequently too much space between shelves. This is a wicked combination, forcing you to create piles in front of piles. The key is in the folding. (See "Folding Towels" on page 47, "Folding Flat Sheets" on page 49, "Folding Fitted Sheets" on page 50, and "Folding Pillowcases" on page 50.)

As with clothes closets, there are three options for organizing your linen closet: custom, handyman, and do-it-yourself. Custom linen closets require a closet company to replace the interior space of the closet with adjustable shelving, creating a clean new look. A handyman can add additional shelves and/or re-set the current shelves, leaving less space between each shelf. Do-it-yourself linen closets are the least expensive. You create them yourself using organizing tools. You can also install ClosetMaid ShelfTrack systems easily and inexpensively yourself. Follow the installation directions provided by ClosetMaid.

CREATING A DO-IT-YOURSELF LINEN CLOSET

 TOTAL TIME:
2 to 4 hours

● **DEGREE OF DIFFICULTY:**
easy

TOOLS:
medium and/or large stacking shelves, Life Liner shelf liner, and baskets

1. Measure the width and depth of each shelf.

2. Measure the space between shelves.

Beverly Hills Top Tip

Put a label on more than one side of storage baskets. This way, if a basket is placed back on the shelf sideways or backwards, there is still a good chance that one of the labels will be visible.

3. Purchase medium and/or large stacking shelves to fit the specs of the measurements in Steps 1 and 2. Stacking shelves are the perfect size to organize this area. The idea here is to create an additional shelf, allowing more space to store items between shelves, and to stop making enormous piles.

4. Empty the linen closet, sorting the items into piles of like items.

5. Line all of the shelves with shelf liner. I recommend Life Liner for its durability, aesthetic appeal, and warranty. Remember that once the liner is cut and placed, that chore is done forever!

6. Fold the towels to fit the entire depth of the space, from the front to back of each shelf, creating long, flat piles. (See "Folding Towels" on page 47.)

7. Place the towels on the shelves, color-coordinated, if you desire.

8. Fold bed linens. (See "Folding Flat Sheets" on page 50, "Folding Fitted Sheets" on page 50, and "Folding Pillowcases" on page 50.) Store linens as sets, with the pillowcases, flat sheets, and fitted sheets together, or store flat and fitted sets together and the pillowcases separately. Roll lesser-used linens and place them on a higher shelf, stored upright inside baskets.

9. Place the linens on the shelves, color-coordinated if you desire.

10. Contain all other miscellaneous items, sorted into piles of like items, inside baskets. Label the baskets and place them on the shelves.

ORGANIZING A HALLWAY CLOSET

Hallway closets are always too small and stuffed with too much stuff. In most hallway closets, there is a shelf above the rod. The space from the shelf to the ceiling can be as much as three feet—that's three feet of space for shoving and piling. The critical thing to do in this situation is to create more shelving in the closet.

 TOTAL TIME:
60 to 90 minutes

● **DEGREE OF DIFFICULTY:**
easy

TOOLS:
medium and large stacking shelves

1. Purchase medium and long stacking shelves to customize the top shelf in the closet. Measure the space between the shelf and the ceiling. Measure the length of the shelf. The height and width of the space will determine how many stacking shelves are required to customize this area.

2. Remove all of the items from the closet and sort them into piles of like items.

3. Install the stacking shelves.

4. Return the items to the closet.

With a handyman's help, I converted an ordinary coat closet into a music-storage area.

CUSTOMIZING CLOSETS

In this section, I'm talking about modifying or creating closets to meet special needs, rather than having a luxurious custom-closet designed by a professional closet company. You can customize any closet or space for specific needs. For example, I gave a coat closet a design makeover to hold stereo equipment and CDs. The closet was then built by a handyman.

Of course, sometimes a closet company is the best answer, as in the case of a client who was trying to operate a business out of her home. Before a buffet workspace was designed and installed by a closet company, the homeowner used her dining room table to make accessories for her home-based business. The area under the window was dead space. The buffet was designed to hold supplies, and the countertop gives my client a large, usable work surface. Best of all, the buffet also doubles as a real buffet, too. (See photo on page 168)

Another example is a space-saving storage system I designed around a refrigerator. I designed it to create more shelving in the kitchen, and fill in the dead space on both sides of the refrigerator. It modernized the look of the refrigerator and gave the homeowner much-needed space.

Occasionally, you will see a master bedroom built in the 1920s or 1930s that has two small closets. These closets were the origins of the first separate "his and hers" closets. However, in the "good old days," women did not have the amount of clothing they have today. A woman could get by on a babushka, an apron, and one pair of shoes. Not true today! If the two closets are connected by a common wall, consider breaking out the wall to create one large closet. You will maximize your space and create a whole new world of storage.

PASADENA CLOSETS

"Pasadena" is the name of a particular closet style that was built sometime between the 1950s and '60s. The Pasadena closet does not function well in this day and age. It can be found in one of two styles: upper cabinets and lower drawers, with the closet space in the center, or upper cabinets with the closet below. Either combination spells disaster for the modern homeowner.

My instincts always go into "destroy" mode when I walk into a room with a Pasadena closet.

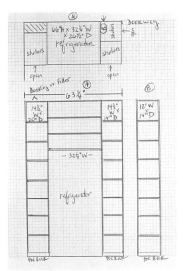

I created a custom shelving system around the refrigerator in this kitchen, to fill what is usually just dead space.

However, I have discovered a way to keep the outer integrity of the cabinetry while creating more space behind the closed doors.

The remedy requires a handyman, but if you have a Pasadena closet, it is well worth the trouble. Empty the closet area and the upper cabinets. I refer to the upper cabinet area as "Siberia space." Generally it is a two-foot-deep wasteland, into which stuff has been shoved and then forgotten about, more than likely ready for the donation truck. Gut

the shelf between the closet and the upper cabinet, leaving an open space from the closet area to the ceiling. By doing this, you have created a higher ceiling in your closet, allowing for double hanging or extra shelving. (See "Closet Design 101" on page 53 for more closet storage solutions.)

OUTSIDE STORAGE CLOSETS

Storage closets are a great addition to any home. The biggest problem with these areas is that they are either big spaces without shelves, or, if there are shelves, there are too few of them. So people end up stacking and piling boxes on top of each other. The boxes become crushed. And, of course, my pet peeve: The boxes are usually poorly labeled, if they're labeled at all.

These problems can be solved easily and inexpensively by using a number of different tools. ClosetMaid has wire shelving on a track system called ShelfTrack. It is easy to install, and the shelves are adjustable. Other solutions include metal shelving units, which are sometimes called gorilla shelves. They're very strong, metal, bookcase-type shelving. Or you can buy durable plastic units. A variety of plastic cabinets and utility shelves that can do the trick are also available.

A built-in nook in this hallway was converted into precious storage space. Used to hold jewelry and accessories and covered for privacy with a roman shade, the hallway nook is the perfect solution. Let your creativity flow. There is space everywhere! Go find it!

I transformed this Pasadena closet to make use of every inch of space.

Beverly Hills Top Tip

If the space permits, create a "library" environment by putting shelves in rows, including the center section of the space.

Organizing Storage Closets

TOTAL TIME:
2 to 4 hours (depending on the size of the closet)

DEGREE OF DIFFICULTY:
moderate (due to the assembly of tools)

TOOLS:
depending on your needs, may include ShelfTrack, gorilla shelves, plastic storage cabinets, utility shelving, Rafter Solutions, and clear plastic storage containers

1. Measure the length, width, and ceiling height of the area.

2. Purchase your organizing tools. Depending on your needs and tastes, these may include ShelfTrack, gorilla shelves, plastic storage cabinets, utility shelving, rafter solutions, and clear plastic storage containers.

3. Remove all of the items from the storage closet and sort them into piles of like items.

4. If any items are currently stored inside cardboard boxes, transfer the items into clear plastic containers and label each container with its contents.

5. Install the organizing tools, following the directions on the tool packages for assembly.

6. Return the filled storage containers and remaining items to the closet shelving.

A ROLLOUT CART MAKES IT EASY TO STORE
AND REACH LAUNDRY SUPPLIES.

Chapter 7

Laundry

While we're on the subject of clothes, let's talk about the laundry. High-traffic areas like laundry rooms need a high level of efficiency. Frequently, cabinet space in these areas is limited and deep, making it difficult to find and store items. Often it is easier to simply leave things out instead of neatly returning them to their places.

If there is enough vertical space, considering retiring the side-by-side washer and dryer and replacing them with a stacking unit. Stacking washer-dryers are excellent, due to their space-saving design, which frees up floor space to install cabinets. Remember, everything looks neater when it is behind closed doors. If you can see it, odds are it looks cluttered.

Since laundry room spaces are different in houses, condos, and apartments, I've provided a variety of options to fit the various needs and available space. Choose the suggestions that apply to your laundry room.

ORGANIZING LAUNDRY ROOMS

TOTAL TIME:
2 to 4 hours

●● DEGREE OF DIFFICULTY:
easy to moderate

TOOLS:
depending on your situation, may include shelves, baskets, rolling ironing organizer, pull-outs, custom-made cabinets, ironing organizer center, wall-mounted drying rack, and rolling laundry basket with attached clothing rod

1. First, evaluate the space. Do you have a side-by-side washer and dryer? Is there space above them? If so, install a shelf and place frequently used items inside baskets on the shelf. If space permits, purchase a rolling ironing organizer to fit between the two machines. It easily slides out when products are needed and tucks back in when not in use.

2. Check out your cabinets. Are they deep-shelved cabinets? Install pull-outs to bring the products out to you for easy reach and a bird's-eye view. (See "Installing Pull-Outs" on page 88.) If you need more cabinet space, consider designing custom cabinets or purchasing ready-made cabinets.

Organize your cabinets to use the space more efficiently. Turn to the Kitchens chapter and read the section on cabinet space (see page 83). Rework the areas that need help in your laundry room by following those instructions, using laundry room products instead of the kitchen items mentioned.

3. Look at your walls. Do you have any unused wall space? Install an ironing organizer center where the ironing board, iron, and cans of spray starch, and oher items can be neatly displayed and housed. Install a wall-mounted drying rack to avoid taking up floor space.

4. Do you have extra floor space? Using a rolling laundry basket with an attached clothing rod attached saves space and keeps clothing wrinkle-free until you can return it to the appropriate closets.

PART THREE

* * * * *

All Around the House

AN ORGANIZED KITCHEN IS AS MUCH A PLEASURE TO
LOOK AT (AND LIVE IN) AS IT IS TO USE.

Chapter 8

Kitchens

The kitchen is the heart of the home. It's also the heart of home-based chaos. Between the rush to prepare meals, everybody dropping stuff hither and yon on their way through the room or in search of a snack, and all the other things kitchens get used as—craft centers, homework stations, and home offices— it's all too easy for kitchens to become Clutter Central. Not to mention *parts* of kitchens—like refrigerators, cabinets, and drawers. (Where *did* those measuring spoons go?!)

Don't despair. It is possible to create a beautiful, well-organized kitchen that's a pleasure to use and spend time in. Let's not waste another second before getting started!

KITCHEN CABINETS

There are two types of kitchen cabinets: uppers (above the countertop) and lowers (below the countertop). Uppers are generally 12" to 14" deep, and lowers are usually 22" to 24" deep. Unless you have a new or recently remodeled kitchen, you'll find the same problems in these two areas in every home. We'll talk about each in turn.

Upper Cabinets

The standard space between upper cabinet shelves is 12". However, a drinking glass is only 6" inches high, leaving 6" of empty space between the top of the glass and the shelf above it. The empty space forces you to stack in order to fill the cabinet. I call the 6" of wasted space "dead space" or "karate space." (In this area, you can do Kung Fu and never knock anything over.)

In newer homes, the shelves are likely adjustable, but often there are not enough shelves to readjust them to your specific needs. An easy remedy in newer homes is to install additional shelves. Regardless, in all homes, new and old, upper cabinets function best when tools are used. Here's a project to help you make the most of them.

STORING DISHES, MUGS, AND CUPS

Stacking and unstacking dishes is a pain. It can take longer to get down a dish than to prepare a meal! Eventually, you may even give up and use paper plates.

 TOTAL TIME:
30 to 40 minutes (per shelf)

● **DEGREE OF DIFFICULTY:**
easy

TOOLS:
china rack (holds up to 10 place settings), corner stacking shelf, slide-on cup holders, slide-on mug holders, and shelf liner

OPTIONAL TOOLS:
undershelf placemat holder and storage keepers

1. Measure the inside of the cabinet. Write down the width and depth of each shelf and the distance between shelves.

2. Remove the china, dishes, cups, and mugs from the cabinet, sorting them into piles of like items.

3. Take inventory of the items in the cabinet, for example, ten mugs, five cups, ten bowls, and ten plates.

4. Purchase your organizing tools: a china rack, corner stacking shelf, slide-on cup holder, and slide-on mug holder.

Note: Slide-on tools have three functions: aesthetic appeal, convenience, and eliminating dead space, creating more useable space.

5. Cut shelf liner and place it on the shelves.

6. Install the china rack, corner stacking shelf, slide-on cup holder, and slide-on mug holder. (Some kitchen cabinets have a partition between the cabinet doors, which can hinder your ability to install your tools. Install each tool on an angle to get it placed on the shelf.) Above..

7. Return all of the items to the cabinet, placing them on the tools.

8. If you currently store your placemats in a drawer, slide an undershelf placemat holder onto a shelf instead. This will free up some drawer space and eliminate more dead space in your upper cabinets.

9. To protect dishes and glasses that you don't use often, store them inside storage keepers.

Beverly Hills Top Tip

Add additional shelves to create more space, help eliminate excess stacking, and to make it more convenient overall.

STORING GLASSES
(DRINKING AND WINE)

TOTAL TIME:
20 to 25 minutes (per shelf)

DEGREE OF DIFFICULTY:
moderate (due to stemware holder installation)

TOOLS:
shelf liner, helper shelves, and stemware holders

1. Measure the inside of the cabinet. Write down the width and depth of each shelf and the distance between shelves.

2. Remove the glasses from the cabinet, sorting like items together.

3. Take inventory of the items, for example, fifteen drinking glasses, fifteen juice glasses, and twenty wine glasses.

4. Purchase organizing tools.

5. Cut the shelf liner and place it on the shelf.

6. Install the helper shelves.

7. Place the glasses below and on top of the helper shelves by making rows of like items from the back of the cabinet to the front. (You can use helper shelves to store cups and mugs, too, instead of slide-on cup and mug holders.)

8. Install the stemware holders to hang wine glasses. Be prepared: They take time to install and require a screwdriver and possibly a hand drill.

9. Hang the wine glasses from the stemware holders in rows of like items from the back of the cabinet to the front.

Beverly Hills Top Tip

I like to use stemware holders because they prevent dust from getting inside glasses. They also help protect glasses from being knocked over and damaged.

Take photos of your organized food areas and put them inside the cabinet doors to help you stay organized when you use and replace objects. You'll never forget where everything goes!

Beverly Hills Top Tip

Once everything has a place and is in place, take a photograph of the space and attach it to the inside of the cabinet. This will remind you where everything goes when you replace items back on the shelves.

Storing Food

It is common to keep food on an upper cabinet shelf, especially if you do not have a pantry area. Here are some ways to store it.

TOTAL TIME:
1 to 2 hours (per upper cabinet)

DEGREE OF DIFFICULTY:
easy

TOOLS:
shelf liner, two-tier lazy susan, baskets, cupboard clips, lazy susan, helper shelves, acrylic shelf organizers, expand-a-shelves, and clear airtight food containers

OPTIONAL TOOLS:
drawer liner or expandable spice organizer

1. Measure the inside of the cabinet. Write down the width and depth of each shelf and the distance between shelves.

2. Empty the cabinet into piles of like items, such as pasta, tea, cereal, and spices.

3. Take inventory of the items.

4. Purchase your organizing tools.

5. Check expiration dates and discard old products. If necessary, start a grocery list to replace discarded items.

6. Cut shelf liner and place it on the shelf.

7. To organize spices, install a two-tier lazy susan and place your spices on it with the labels facing out. Spin the lazy susan around and view all your spices at once. If you prefer, alphabetize them for added convenience.

8. Store small, loose packages or boxes of teas, rice, puddings, and other items, inside a basket. Place them upright so that their labels are visible. Baskets keep smaller items contained and convenient. Pull the basket off the shelf, take out what you need, and replace it on the shelf.

9. Attach cupboard clips to the inside door of the cabinet with sticky tape. Place packets of dip, dressing, gravy, and drink mixes under the clips with the labels facing out.

10. Put bottles of oil, cooking spray, vinegar, and other liquids on a lazy susan with all labels facing out.

11. Place helper shelves on shelves to double the shelf space. Place boxed items (such as cake mixes, potato buds, rice, and macaroni) on the helper shelves on their sides with the labels facing out, all in the same direction.

12. Store canned goods one of three ways: on a helper shelf, acrylic shelf organizer, or expand-a-shelf and place like items from back to front. The acrylic shelf and expand-a-shelf are great for elevating the items on the back of the shelf. No more repeat purchasing of food you own but could not see!

13. Transfer the contents of opened boxes or bags of food to clear, airtight food containers. The containers will keep the food fresh longer, saving you money in the long run, and they'll also help you keep track of how much of each item is left. Looking through a clear plastic container is the best way to see when you need to make a trip to the grocery store.

14. Return the items to the cabinet, keeping like items together.

Here's a spice drawer alternative: Purchase a drawer liner or an expandable spice and seasoning organizer (top). Arrange spices alphabetically and admire your work!

LOWER CABINETS

Lower cabinets have deep space: two feet for digging and searching. Many newer and remodeled homes have drawers that pull out in the lower cabinets. If yours don't, however, you can customize your kitchen by installing pull-outs. The purpose of a pull-out is to bring the shelf out to you, giving you a bird's-eye view of the contents. Imagine: No more reaching in, digging, and searching!

If installing pull-outs isn't an option for you, you'll find alternate solutions for lower-cabinet organizing on the following pages.

INSTALLING PULL-OUTS

Pots and pans, food storage containers, appliances, cookie cutters, and cooking products are all great items to store in pull-outs, which you install within a lower cabinet.

 TOTAL TIME:
30 to 60 minutes (per pull-out)

●●● **DEGREE OF DIFFICULTY:**
moderate to difficult (depending on the level of handyman skills)

 TOOLS:
pull-out shelves

1. Measure the length and width of your shelf. The cabinet may be wide enough to install two pull-outs side by side.

2. Purchase pull-out(s).

3. Empty the contents of the shelf, sorting them into piles of like items.

4. Follow the directions for installation provided with the pull-out.

5. Return the items to the shelf by placing them upright inside of the pull-out.

6. If space permits, place corresponding lids on the pots and pans.

CREATING MORE
DEEP-SPACE SOLUTIONS

⏱ **TOTAL TIME:**
30 to 45 minutes (per shelf)

● **DEGREE OF DIFFICULTY:**
easy

∧ **TOOLS:**
depending on the contents of the cabinet, may include baskets (for storing small items) frying pan rack, plastic lid holder, and bakeware rack

▲ **OPTIONAL TOOLS:**
hanging pot and pan rack and tension rods

1. Measure the length and width of each shelf in the cabinet.

2. Empty the cabinet, sorting the items into piles of like items.

3. Take inventory of the items.

4. Purchase tools.

5. Store low-use appliances in the rear of the cabinet, with baskets and racks in the front. Or reverse placement, with high-use appliances located in the front and baskets and racks in the rear.

Beverly Hills Top Tip

Tension rods are another solution to keep items upright. Secured between shelves, tension rods are an inexpensive, handy solution.

Beverly Hills Top Tip

Another solution for storing pots and pans is to install a hanging pot and pan rack over the stove, sink, table, or kitchen island. This is a great way to get a decorative look combined with a space-saving function.

6. Install a frying pan rack in the rear of the cabinet, with the handles pointing straight out towards the door. This will keep you from having to stack and un stack your pans. Reach in, pull a pan out, and slide it back in when not in use. It's that easy!

7. Gather all of your plastic lids in a plastic lid holder. Another option is to store the lids on the containers. This is actually my favorite option. It's one of the only times I approve of stacking. Stack similar-sized containers together.

8. Given the generous amount of space between shelves and the ample depth of lower cabinets, install one or more bakeware racks side by side. Place cookie sheets and platters upright in the racks. No more stacking and unstacking; no more dead space. Pull out your platters and cookie sheets with one-motion ease.

Beverly Hills Top Tip

Baskets are an inexpensive and convenient alternative to pull-out shelves. Items stored in baskets are grouped, contained, and easily accessible. Reach into the cabinet, pull out the basket, remove what you need, and replace the basket on shelf. Simple! No more knocking items around and creating chaos inside the cabinets during the process.

ORGANIZING UNDER THE SINK

The space under sinks is desperately needed and frequently underutilized. To double the useable space under all sinks, install under-sink shelves. The beauty of these shelves is that they expand to the width of the cabinet, and the shelves adjust to fit around the plumbing.

 TOTAL TIME:
30 to 60 minutes

●● **DEGREE OF DIFFICULTY:**
easy to moderate

⚖ **TOOLS:**
expandable under-sink storage shelf and cabinet door kitchen wrap rack

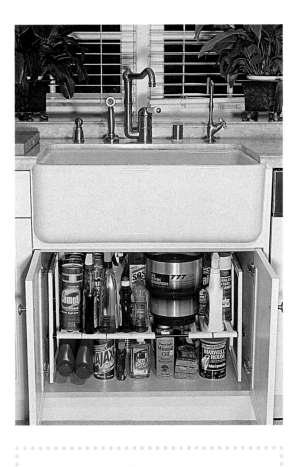

1. Remove all items from under the sink, sorting them into piles of like items.

2. Prior to assembling the expandable under-sink storage shelf, determine if you will need to use one or two of the shelves provided with the product. To do this, look at the height of the products you will be storing under the sink. Generally, I use one shelf in kitchen installations and two shelves in bathrooms. Kitchen cleaning products are much taller than the types of things most people store under bathroom sinks, requiring more space.

   Use your tallest product as your guide to the figure placement of the shelves. Hold the product next to the side support. Insert one end of the pole into the hole that clears the top of the product. Follow the directions for assembly.

3. Return products to under the sink, placing them on the shelves.

Beverly Hills Top Tip

Assemble under-sink storage shelves right inside the cabinet. Otherwise, they won't fit properly

4. If you currently store plastic wrap and aluminum foil in a drawer, free up the drawer by installing a cabinet door kitchen wrap rack to the inside the cabinet door. Stash the plastic wrap and aluminum foil there, instead.

PANTRIES

Pantries are like closets; they can be walk-in or reach-in. Both types have challenges.

Reach-in pantries are usually five-foot-tall kitchen cabinets that are two feet deep. The average person has the shelves packed like a trash compactor. More than likely the stuff in the middle to the back of each shelf is old and stale. I call the deep space in pantries Siberia. It's far away and rarely visited. The deep space needs to be accessible. This can be done by using the appropriate tools, which will create more space, accessibility, and function.

Walk-in pantries are generally found in larger homes. Even if you are lucky enough to have one, odds are that things could be better. The most common problem is the depth of the shelves. They are either too deep or too shallow. Another issue is the distance between shelves. We'll tackle this problem in the pantry organizing project on the next page.

Beverly Hills Top Tip

When you've poured your cereal out into plastic storage containers, don't just toss the cardboard boxes. First, check for recipes you may want to keep. For example: If you want to keep the Rice Krispies treat recipe, cut it out, insert it into a Ziploc bag, and toss the bag inside the container with the cereal.

Organizing Pantries

⏱ **TOTAL TIME:**
3 to 5 hours
(based on a reach-in pantry with five shelves)

●● **DEGREE OF DIFFICULTY:**
moderate

✗ **TOOLS:**
depending on the contents of the pantry, may include clear plastic food containers, helper shelves, expand-a-shelf, two-tier lazy susan, wire baskets, cupboard clips, kitchen wrap rack, and bakeware organizer

⚹ **OPTIONAL TOOLS:**
pull-out shelves and placemat holder

1. Empty the contents of the pantry, sorting them into piles of like items.

2. Check the products' expiration dates and discard any stale products. If necessary, start a grocery list to replace discarded items.

3. Pour the contents of any opened packages into clear plastic food containers. Label each container. Even though the container is clear, the label will identify the type of food inside. It also looks great.

4. Measure the width and depth of the pantry shelves and the amount of space between shelves so that you can determine how many tools will fit inside the pantry.

5. If your pantry shelves are adjustable, adjust them and purchase more shelves. To readjust the shelves, you can start at either the top or bottom. Install each shelf as close to the next shelf as possible, allowing the tallest item that you plan to keep on the shelf to fit.

6. Purchase organizing tools.

7. Place the tools inside the pantry to make the best fit. Install helper shelves and expand-a-shelves in the back of the pantry shelves where canned goods and boxed items will be stored. Some shelves may require two helper shelves side by side, an expand-a-shelf and a helper shelf side by side, or perhaps just an expand-a-shelf. This is your masterpiece; have fun and work with the tools that meet your needs.

8. Place your food on the new tools, for example, canned goods on expand-a-shelves and boxed goods on helper shelves. Remember, if a box doesn't fit upright, turn it on its side.

9. Place small items, such as spices, on a two-tier lazy susan on the right or left side of a shelf. Place items on the lazy susan, with their labels facing out. Spin the lazy susan around and view all your spices at once. You can alphabetize them for added convenience.

10. Gather small items and place them in wire baskets. Place the baskets on the shelves in front of the tools. This serves several purposes: Baskets contain smaller items, they're easy to handle, it's easy to remove an entire basket to reach items stored in back of cabinet, and it brings all items out for a bird's-eye view, leaving no more wasted space.

11. If you have a deep cabinet, consider installing pull-outs on the bottom shelves. (See "Installing Pull-Outs" on page 88.)

12. Attach cupboard clips to your pantry door to hold items such as spice packets.

13. Install a kitchen wrap rack to the door of your pantry to hold plastic wrap and free up the drawer in which you've likely been storing them.

Continued on next page

14. If you currently keep your placemats in a drawer, consider installing a placemat holder on a pantry shelf. This uses up some dead space in the pantry and frees up the drawer. Add a bakeware rack, if desired, to store bakeware items.

15. Return all of the items to the pantry, keeping like items together.

COUNTERTOPS

Do I need to remind you how kitchens appear in the pages of your favorite design magazines? There's no clutter of any kind! To get that designer look in your own kitchen, keep the appliances and knickknacks on your countertop down to a bare minimum. Keep only the items with high-frequency use on your countertop. Store medium- to lower-use appliances in lower cabinets or in the pantry, keeping your countertop bare.

Beverly Hills Top Tip

I am not a fan of bulletin boards in general, but if they're used properly in a kitchen (as in this photo), they can look more like a framed piece of art rather than an ordinary bulletin board. They're a great place to put the stuff that usually ends up all over the refrigerator door!

Trolleys and Islands

What do you do if your kitchen is organized, but you still need more space? Consider purchasing a kitchen trolley or island. These are portable tables on wheels. Many islands come with additional features, such as paper-towel and dish-towel holders, drawers, wine racks, and trays. They make a design statement and provide a little more room to spread out.

Imagine the joy of having clutter-free counters to unload groceries on and extra room to prepare meals. However, before this new reality can materialize, you've got to begin organizing on the inside. Not until you have organized everything inside your drawers and behind cabinet doors can the countertops get cleared.

REFRIGERATORS

If refrigerator doors had counters, they could tell us how many times we were in them on a daily, weekly, or even annual basis. Even though we open the refrigerator door more often than any other door in the kitchen, the need to organize this space seems to be forgotten.

Here are five points to consider when organizing the refrigerator:

1. Door swing. Does your refrigerator door open on the right or left side? Is it convenient with the current swing? Doors can easily be re-hung for your convenience. The entire process takes about one hour.

2. Space next to the refrigerator. Is there space to the left or right of your refrigerator? You can install shelves around the refrigerator. This can increase your kitchen space and give a great custom design feel. (See the photo on page 73. I created a custom shelving system around the refrigerator in that kitchen to make use of what was previously dead space.)

3. Shelving material. Do you have wire shelves inside your refrigerator? You can purchase clear shelf liner designed to go on top of wire shelving, or you can have acrylic or Lucite pieces cut to fit your shelves. It will update your refrigerator and make the shelves easier to clean.

4. Shelf spacing. Did you know that the shelves in your refrigerator are adjustable? Re-adjust the shelves to suit your needs.

5. Door art. Do you have art, magnets, and clutter covering your refrigerator? De-clutter the kitchen by starting with the refrigerator. Less is so much more!

Organizing the Refrigerator

 TOTAL TIME:
2 hours (refrigerator contents only)

●●● **DEGREE OF DIFFICULTY:**
easy to difficult
(depending on the five points listed on page 95)

TOOLS:
shelf liners or acrylic or Lucite pieces, wire baskets, plastic baskets, lazy susan, beverage dispenser, baking-soda caddy, condiment caddy, starter sets, and freezer shelves (stackable helper shelves made for the freezer)

1. Consider the direction in which your refrigerator door opens, to the left or to the right. If it's not convenient, switch it!

2. Check to see if there's any extra space next to your refrigerator. If you can add some small shelves in there, do it.

3. Empty the refrigerator and freezer, discarding stale items and sorting items into piles of like items.

4. Check out your refrigerator shelves. If they are wire shelves, place clear shelf liners on top, or have acrylic or Lucite pieces cut to fit your shelves.

5. Consider the shelf spacing. Move shelves up or down to maximize your space and still fit the tallest items in. For example, leave enough space above the top shelf to accommodate milk cartons.

6. Use wire baskets to organize your freezer. Baskets make it easier to access food and cut down on the risk of waste. Store food items upright in baskets with product labels facing out. Baskets are excellent in both side-by-side and top-loading freezers.

7. Place plastic baskets inside the refrigerator's fruit and vegetable bins to keep items from rolling all over each other and bruising.

8. Store cheeses and meats inside baskets, too. This way, when you're preparing meals, all sandwich goodies will be together and can be easily removed in one swoop.

9. Place a lazy susan on a shelf and put back your jellies, jars, and other small condiment containers on it, with their labels facing out. Now spin it around and see all the contents at once.

10. Place a beverage dispenser on a shelf to hold canned drinks and provide easy roll-out convenience.

11. To help prevent odors, place a box of opened baking soda inside a baking-soda caddy. You'll eliminate the risk of spilling the soda; the caddy attaches to a shelf.

12. Place condiments that you use often in a condiment caddy. This makes them easy to remove from the refrigerator to the table in one easy step Ideally, place the condiment caddy on a door shelf.

13. Install starter sets on the refrigerator shelves. Starter sets are similar to helper shelves. Install them by attaching them to the side of a shelf and double up your space. Place freezer shelves in the freezer.

14. Return all items to the refrigerator and freezer, keeping like items together and placing items that you use most up front and on the door shelves. Place items that you use less often toward the back of the refrigerator and freezer.

KITCHEN PAPERWORK

Many people, especially those without home offices, store paperwork in their kitchens. This can be handy because we spend so much time in our kitchens.

Some fortunate individuals have small areas in their kitchens that serve as desks. Countless others use their kitchen countertops to spread out their bills and other paperwork. They need a place to store all that paper. Having a file cabinet in the kitchen is not practical unless it is already part of the desk area. But you can create hidden filing space simply and inexpensively. Here's how.

STORING KITCHEN PAPERWORK

🕐 **TOTAL TIME:**
45 to 60 minutes (per shelf)

●● **DEGREE OF DIFFICULTY:**
moderate

⅄ **TOOLS:**
plastic file crates to hold letter- or legal-size files (or cardboard file boxes or file frames) and pull-out drawer

1. Choose a lower cabinet to store paperwork that is wide enough to accommodate one or two file crates side-by-side. This means you will be giving up some kitchen storage space to make room for files.

Note: The crates are made of plastic, so they can be trimmed down without losing the hanging space. It may be necessary to trim if the crate's width is a little wider than your cabinet's width.

2. Install a pull-out drawer unless your shelf has a custom pull-out. (See "Pull-Out Installation" on page 88.)

3. Place the file crates, frames, or boxes on the pull-out drawer.

4. Put files inside the crate. (We'll talk more about actually organizing the paperwork later in the book in chapter 13, Home Offices.)

A WELL-DESIGNED AND ORDERLY BEDROOM IS A
BEAUTIFUL, PEACEFUL RETREAT

Chapter 9

Bedrooms

Bedrooms should be our most tranquil places. No clutter of any kind should fill this space. For a bedroom to be clear of clutter, the closets, drawers, and armoires *must* be organized.

Follow the steps I've provided in "Closets" (beginning on page 53) and "Drawers, Drawers, and More Drawers" (beginning on page 31). Expanding your bedroom organizing efforts by clever design and the use of tools enables you to further contain and organize any remaining items that are still visible to the eye. Here are my suggestions for four of these areas or objects: the entertainment area, nightstands, bedroom offices, and jewelry.

THE ENTERTAINMENT AREA

Televisions are best hidden whenever possible. Purchasing an armoire or entertainment center lets you hide the television—and all those unsightly cables—when you're not watching it. Plus, an armoire or entertainment center will give the room height and interesting design lines.

But be smart before purchasing *any* furniture item. Measure your television, stereo equipment, DVD player, and other electronics. to make sure all items will fit. Before buying a piece of furniture consider whether or not it has plenty of drawer space to store CDs and other gear. You can also create your own custom design and have a closet company or contractor build the piece.

NIGHTSTANDS

Small bedside tables, or nightstands, are standard fixtures in most bedrooms. Nightstands with drawers need drawer organizers inside to keep all those bits and pieces within easy reach. (See "Drawers, Drawers, and More Drawers" beginning on page 31 for more on drawer organizers.) If you are considering purchasing new furniture, be sure the nightstands you buy have drawers, unless you have another option to store your personal "stuff."

Nightstands are perfect for containing all that essential bedtime clutter, from reading glasses to an alarm clock. Put lamps on them to bring more light to the bed area.

BEDROOM OFFICES

Many homes I visit have home offices in bedrooms. Let me state here: If there is business in the bedroom, there won't be any "monkey business" going on! Move any office stuff—desk, paper, and bills—out of the bedroom. If you don't have a whole room dedicated to your office, I recommend moving the office area to the corner of a living room or dining room instead. Generally, more hours are spent in the bedroom than any other room in the house, and it should be kept as a peaceful area where anything associated with stress is not welcome.

JEWELRY

Jewelry trays are some of my favorite ways to organize and store jewelry. There are a variety of trays available, for earrings, bracelets, necklaces, rings, and watches. The trays are stackable and can be stored inside a drawer.

Another possibility is upright displays for those who prefer to keep their jewelry visible and convenient. Do you collect glasses? There are even sunglass and eyeglass displays.

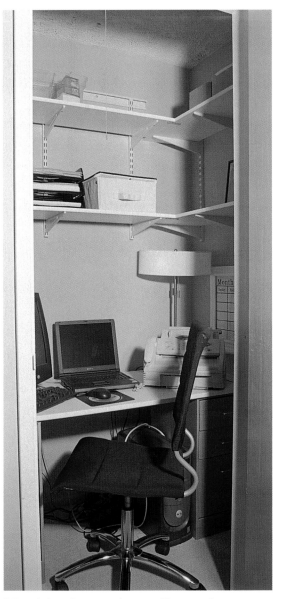

My advice: Get your home office *out* of your bedroom! In this case, it was moved into a convenient closet.

THE BATHROOM SHOULD BE A BEAUTIFUL,
INVITING PART OF YOUR HOME.

Chapter 10

Bathrooms

One of the most challenging areas for many people to organize is the bathroom. With the dozens of products and appliances we use in the bathroom, it is understandable that space is running low. This forces many people to use their countertops and shower floors as two more storage spaces, leaving bathrooms a cluttered mess. The key is to rework and maximize the available room by using tools create more space where there appears to be none. With a little Houdini know-how, it's time to create some organizing magic.

Whether small or spacious, a well-organized bathroom space is as attractive as it is practical. Note these clutter-free counters!

ORGANIZING BATHROOMS

TOTAL TIME:
3 to 4 hours
(for a small- to medium-size bathroom)

DEGREE OF DIFFICULTY:
easy

TOOLS:
depending on the types of items you store in you bathroom, may include expandable drawer liners, Drawer Doublers, Cosmetic Stax, Face Space cosmetics organizer, lipstick organizer, pull-out drawers, baskets, expandable under-sink shelf or helper shelf, plastic baskets, lazy susan, over-the-door hook, over-door towel rack, shower dispenser, squeegee, drawer organizers, mini expand-a-shelves, blow-drier holder, and cotton ball and swab holder

OPTIONAL TOOLS:
Life Liner shelf liner, étagère, medicine cabinet shelves, and over-the-tank magazine rack

1. Organize bathrooms from the inside out. Start with the drawers. (See "Drawers, Drawers, and More Drawers" beginning on page 31.) While you're discarding old products and expired medication, follow the instructions for organizing drawers before continuing with Step 2.

There are many choices for bathroom drawer organizers. Line drawers with expandable drawer liners. Bottles will stay put and won't roll around on an expandable drawer liner. Add Drawer Doublers to make your current drawer size about 50 percent larger.

2. Remove all the products under the sink and inside cabinets. Sort products into piles of like items.

3. Install pull-outs or place baskets in deep lower cabinets. The purpose of a pull-out is to bring

Cosmetics

Store makeup in a drawer by using Cosmetic Stax, a type of drawer organizer designed to hold cosmetics such as pencils, eye shadows, and nail polish. Use acrylic organizers, a cosmetic organizer, or Face Space cosmetics organizer when drawer space is limited.

How many lipsticks do you have? Use a lipstick organizer and place lipsticks inside the organizer with the name of color facing up.

Place cosmetics inside cosmetic organizers and store them under the sink, in a cabinet, or in an étagère.

the shelf out to you, giving you a bird's-eye view of the contents. Imagine no more reaching in, digging, and searching! Baskets can also be used in conjunction with pull-outs or by themselves. Place products inside baskets and store them on a cabinet shelf. Simply reach for a basket, place it on the countertop, retrieve the items you need, and replace it on its shelf. (See "Pull-Out Installation" on page 88.)

4. If you wish, this is a great time to line cabinets and the under-sink area with Life Liner shelf liner.

5. Optional: To gain additional storage space, consider purchasing an étagère that fits around the toilet or adding more bathroom cabinets. I prefer an étagère that is built like a cabinet instead of open shelving, especially if it will be

7. Use plastic baskets to contain smaller items and bottles that you sorted into piles of like items and place them on an under-sink shelf. Items in baskets are contained and easily accessible. Reach in under the sink, pull out a basket, remove the needed contents, and replace the basket on its shelf. No more knocking items about, no more repeat purchasing, and no more chaos inside the cabinets. Bonus: more storage space = clear bathroom countertops!

Label the baskets for convenience: lotions, feminine products, dental care, bath, for example.

used to store toiletries. Keeping unsightly products out in plain view gives the appearance of clutter.

Cabinets provide additional space, too. They can be purchased in conjunction with the étagère. Cabinets will require assembly and installation so you may need to hire a handyman.

6. Increase your under-sink storage. I prefer to use an expandable under-sink storage shelf. However, in guest bathrooms where storage is not sparse, helper shelves are another option.

Generally, I use two under-sink shelves in bathrooms. Prior to assembling an expandable under-sink storage shelf, determine the height of the products you will be storing under the sink. Use your tallest product as your guide to figure placement of the shelves. Hold the product next to the side support. Insert one end of the pole into the hole that clears the top of the product. Follow the directions for assembly.

Beverly Hills Top Tip

Open shelving is fine for towels, but "stuff" needs to stay behind closed doors and inside drawers.

money. You'll have no more waste by accidentally spilling expensive shampoos down the drain. The buttons dispense just the right amount.

Think about it: One of the pleasures of staying in a hotel is the clutter-free shower, with no bottles of any kind to trip over or slip on.

Just because bathtubs have narrow ledges around them does not justify using that surface to keep more stuff. Store all bath items inside a cabinet or under the sink.

12. Get a squeegee. Water spots on shower doors and walls caused by water and steam left to drip dry add to the unappealing look of disorganization. Once the bathroom is organized, eyes will then focus on the dirty glass. Get in the habit of using a squeegee after each shower. It will leave your glass and shower walls spot-free, giving you a fresh shower to step into each time you use it.

13. If you have a medicine cabinet with extra slots for shelves, purchase more shelves. You can purchase additional shelves at a Home Depot or Lowe's store. This will cut down on the dead space.

14. Organize small items in the medicine cabinet in drawer organizers. This keeps them contained and easier to reach without knocking over other products in the process.

Mini expand-a-shelves are another option to eat up the dead space. By creating two tiers per shelf, they double the shelf size.

15. If you read in the bathroom, purchase an over-the-tank magazine rack that holds books, and magazines. Lift the tank top, slide the bracket, attach the basket, and it is installed.

8. Place a lazy susan on a shelf under the sink for easy viewing of products.

9. Place an over-the-door hook on the inside of the bathroom door to hang robes. No installation is required.

10. Place an over-the-door towel rack over the bathroom door or shower door on which to hang towels.

11. Eliminate all of those bottles of products in the shower and create a clean look by installing a shower dispenser. If you have more than four products that you use on your hair and body, install a second dispenser. Dispensers not only eliminate unsightly bottles, they also save you

16. Store bathroom appliances, such as a flat iron, blow dryer, crimper, curling iron, in a cabinet or under the sink, if possible. Or you can purchase a blow-dryer holder and attach it to the wall. This way your appliances will be accessible, yet contained.

17. If you use an electric toothbrush, store the charger when it's not in use. Keeping the toothbrush in the charger can eventually destroy the battery. Electric toothbrushes need to be charged only about once a month. Storing the charger while not in use also gets one more thing off the countertop.

18. Other than a soap dish or dispenser, tissue box, and cotton balls and swabs, your bathroom countertop should now be clutter-free. Purchase a cotton ball-and-swab holder to store these items.

THIS LIVING ROOM HAS BEEN DESIGNED FOR LIVING—NOT
JUST LOOKING! NOTICE THERE IS NO CLUTTER OF ANY KIND.

Chapter 11

Living Rooms, Dining Rooms, and Family Rooms

The simple rule for living rooms, dining rooms, and family rooms is "Nothing on the floor no more!" But in this case, the rule extends to tabletops and sofas, too. Keep these spaces clutter-free. There *are* solutions to eliminate the clutter! Multipurpose furniture with hidden storage like buffets are one option. Keep "the fresh eye" in mind as you organize these rooms. (See "What You'll Need to Succeed" on page 15.)

Your dining room should welcome family and guests—and that means a clutter-free table!

Practicing the 30-Second Rule in the family room or den is imperative to keep the space organized. Put things away as soon as you are finished using them. Families spend a lot of time in these rooms. They are high-use rooms for entertainment, play, and relaxation. The best way to keep things organized is to have plenty of bookcases, built-in cabinets, and an entertainment center. If you're really fortunate, you have a screening room, too. We'll talk about each of these in turn. Keep remotes contained in a clicker caddy.

BOOKCASES

Bookcases are *not* just for books! Use them to organize videos, DVDs, and CDs, too.

Bookcases can add visual interest to a large wall, and they provide great display and storage space! Make sure you match the bookcase style to your room's style.

ORGANIZING BOOKCASES

 TOTAL TIME:
1 to 2 hours
(per bookcase, depending on the amount of items)

DEGREE OF DIFFICULTY:
easy to moderate (depending on the amount of items and creativity level)

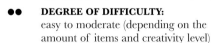 **TOOLS:**
bookends

OPTIONAL TOOLS:
CD, DVD, and video holders

1. Take all items out of the bookcase. Sort books by subject or author.

2. Graduate the sorted books by height, from tallest to shortest.

3. Arrange the books on the shelves vertically and horizontally, creating a designer appearance like you'd see in a magazine. If books fill more than one shelf, alternate the vertical and horizontal placement from shelf to shelf.

4. Use bookends to keep upright books straight.

5. Optional: Occasionally place an accessory on a horizontal stack of books.

6. Sort CDs, DVDs, and videos into piles. Arrange DVDs and videos by type—Disney, comedy, thriller, for example—and arrange music by artist and/or type; alphabetize all.

7. Place the sorted CDs, DVDs, and videos on bookshelves, using bookends to keep them upright if necessary. Optional: Store CDs, DVDs, and videos in a DVD/CD holder, stackable CD holder, or stackable video holder.

BUILT-IN CABINETS

Do you have built-in cabinets in your family room? Built-ins are a bonus; however, most built-ins are underutilized. Like lower kitchen cabinets, the space is generally deep and hard to reach.

Organize this space by following the same format outlined in the "Pull-Out Installation" project on page 88. Many newer and remodeled homes already have pull-outs (custom drawers that replace deep shelves) for the lower cabinets. Now you can also customize your built-in cabinets with pull-outs that you purchase and install yourself. The purpose of a pull-out is to bring the shelf out to you, giving you a bird's-eye view of the contents. Imagine: No more reaching in, digging, and searching!

Baskets serve as alternate solutions to the pull-outs. Items in baskets are contained and easily accessible. You can simply reach into the cabinet, pull out a basket, remove the items you need, and replace the basket on its shelf. No more knocking items around and creating chaos inside the cabinets during the process.

ENTERTAINMENT CENTERS

An entertainment center can hold everything from the stereo equipment, television, and video and DVD recorders to all the movies, music, and, of course, remotes. Consider purchasing an armoire large enough to house all your gear or have an

A beautiful screening room is the ultimate luxury—and the perfect modern family room.

entertainment center custom-designed and built to your specifications. It's worth it—after all, face it, the entertainment center is the focal point in your living room or family room. If you create an entertainment center in an armoire or custom cabinet, you'll find that the best part of all is that when it's not in use, you can close the doors and you'll have a beautiful piece of furniture.

Organize all the items that belong inside the entertainment center as you would organize a bookcase. (See "Bookcases" on page 110.) Some entertainment centers have drawers in which you can store items such as DVDs and video tapes. Place them inside the drawers with all the labels facing up and turned in the same direction. Don't forget to alphabetize them, too!

THE SCREENING ROOM

Screening rooms are the ultimate in luxury. No home organizing book would be complete without a description of one. A screening room is usually equipped with plush seating, a popcorn maker, table, pillow, and blankets for all. Store movies and videos tucked away in drawers or behind closed pull-out cabinets. You are about to relax and see a movie—not a bunch of clutter!

THERE'S NO REASON A CHILD'S ROOM
CAN'T BE FUN *AND* FUNCTIONAL!

Chapter 12

Children's Rooms and Playrooms

Take a moment to think back to the time you were in preschool or kindergarten. Everything in the classroom, including your chair, was big. You could barely reach the hook in your "cubby" space to hang up your jacket without standing on your tiptoes.

Now speed the clock forward and enter your child's preschool classroom as an adult. Everything that was once so big is now so small. You have grown up, and everything is proportionate—to your adult self.

Try seeing space through the eyes of a child; imagine how large a mountain of clutter appears to them, even when it is only a small molehill to you. A big mess to you is equivalent to Mount Everest to them. It is only fair to your children to create an environment for them that is neat and clutter-free. I believe clutter blocks minds from reaching their full potential. Start your children out on a clear playing field. They will enjoy a clutter-free environment as much as you do.

Remember, the gift of organization is one of the greatest gifts you can give your children. Organization is a lifestyle, and begun early, it will

have an enormously positive impact on your childrens' lives—how they view their surroundings, how they treat their belongings and others' belongings, how they conduct themselves, and even how they develop their schoolwork habits. Organization spills over into every aspect of our lives.

FUNCTIONAL FURNITURE

Furniture is a large expenditure. Investing in the right pieces can save a family a small fortune. Purchase furniture that can grow as your child grows.

Start buying smart from day one: Purchase a crib that converts into a small child's bed. This will take your child from infancy to six or seven years of age. When your child is in the second grade, he or she is old enough to move up to a permanent furniture set that will take him or her straight through high school. Race cars and Barbie furniture are *not* good choices! Most likely, those types of purchases will land you back in another furniture store before your kids reach middle school.

Here are a few important factors to consider when buying children's furniture. How large is the room? Are your children sharing a room? Do you plan on having another child who will share a room?

Underbed storage is a great solution for a child's room—or *any* bedroom.

Trundle beds are good for small rooms. They're especially convenient for sleepover guests. Bunk beds with storage drawers are another good choice for room sharing. Custom iron beds can be ordered specifically to your height requirements. High beds are fun; children can use a step stool to climb into bed, and they can use the under-the-bed space for toy storage.

Bookcases are an important furniture choice. They can hold toy containers, help keep things off the floor in the early years, and convert to young adult needs as the years go by.

Purchasing a desk that "works" is of extreme importance. Many people buy desks that look good but don't function well. The best configuration is a desk with many drawers. If a desk is short on drawers, where will the stuff go? Functional desks have a drawer in the center for supplies, such as pens, pencils, markers, erasers, paper clips, scissors, and rulers. There should also be drawers for stationery, miscellaneous items, and files. (See "Drawers,

Drawers, and More Drawers," beginning on page 30, for more on organizing all this.)

The goal: Children should never have to get up from their chairs during the study/homework time. Everything should be at their fingertips inside their desk drawers. Consider shopping for desks at an unfinished furniture store. When I searched for the perfect desk for my daughter, I found it there.

PAPERWORK

Good work habits, when established young, will stay with your children their entire lives. Creating a clean, clutter-free work environment is essential. Teaching your children how to keep it that way is one function of the 30-Second Rule. Put things away in their proper resting place as soon as you're finished using them.

We've already talked about the importance of purchasing a proper desk for your school-age child. It doesn't matter if it appears to be too big for them now. They will grow into it before you know it. Once the desk is in place, fill it with all the supplies they need to do their work. You're trying to create a mini-office, if you will.

Together, help your child make a file system for his or her work. (We'll talk about creating a filing system in more detail in chapter 13, beginning on page 122.) The age of the child does not matter. Even at three and four years old, they have observed you with your papers. When kids are young, paperwork looks like fun! They want to have their papers organized, too. Create files for coloring books, drawings, and certificates or awards for young children. Create subject files for older children, such as English, math, and history.

The concept is what is important here. Developing a healthy relationship with paper and how to deal with it is a gift. When children grow up

Drawer organizers make it easy to keep kids' supplies together and easy to find.

controlling their paperwork instead of being out of control, they are light-years ahead of the others. These simple systems will spill over into their notebooks and school projects.

ORGANIZING ART PROJECTS

Looking at a child's art projects conjures up fond memories of days gone by. The darling handprints and the Thanksgiving turkey plate are all part of our children's formative years. These treasures need to be preserved for many years to come.

As a general rule, always date the back of the "work of art," or write down the grade your child was in when it was made. Years later, it will be fun to look back and know when your child created each masterpiece.

Many people enjoy displaying the art projects in their homes, perhaps taping them on the refrigerator or framing them to hang on a wall. But we only have so much space! When it is time to rotate the work to show off a new piece, it needs to be stored. Here's how.

TOTAL TIME:
5 minutes (if begun from day 1) to hours (if sorting numerous years)

DEGREE OF DIFFICULTY:
easy

TOOLS:
under-the-bed plastic storage drawers or clear plastic containers

1. Purchase under-the-bed plastic storage drawers or clear plastic containers. Label the containers. (Example: Kindergarten, 2004.)

2. Fill the container with your child's treasures.

3. Keep the container under a bed for easy access. When the container is full, add another label. (Example: Through Second Grade, 2006.)

4. Remove each filled container and store it in a more permanent, but safe place, such as a closet or the garage.

5. Repeat steps 1 through 4 as needed.

Beverly Hills Top Tip

Pasta or any food art is best left for leftovers! Save these memories with a photograph.

ORGANIZING SCHOOL PAPERS

Saving children's school papers and book reports are part of being a parent. These are fond memories of school days.

 TOTAL TIME:
5 minutes (if begun from day 1) to hours (if sorting numerous years)

● **DEGREE OF DIFFICULTY:**
easy

TOOLS:
stackable file crate or stackable plastic file drawer and letter-size hanging files

1. Purchase one of the tools and label the outside of the container. (Example: Chase's School Work.)

2. Using hanging files, prepare a main heading tab for each school year. (Example: 1st Grade.)

3. When the container is full, label the outside with the school years it covers.

4. Purchase another container, stack it on top, and repeat steps 1 through 3 as needed.

Beverly Hills Top Tip

If you have more than one child, either purchase additional containers, one for each child, or label each main heading tab with the children's names (example: Joe 1st Grade, Sarah Preschool), and/or differentiate the children's work by color-coding the main heading tabs (Joe – blue, Sarah – red).

Backpacks

Starting from day one, children are required to bring backpacks to school. Time will tell how their backs will hold out after years of carrying heavy backpacks.

To help your children get relief from their backpacks' weight, here are two options: Purchase a backpack with wheels and consider purchasing a second set of books, so they'll have one set for home and one set for school.

Help your child by clearing out anything they may be carrying that adds additional unnecessary weight, such as old papers and extra pens.

Consider purchasing backpacks with several different compartments. This will also help keep your children's belongings organized.

Organizing Lockers

Lockers are narrow upright towers that fill from the bottom to the top. Fortunately, it is possible to purchase many different tools to turn the heap into an organized haven.

 TOTAL TIME:
10 to 30 minutes

● **DEGREE OF DIFFICULTY:**
easy

 **TOOLS:**
stackable Locker Solutions, magnetic mirror, basket, and pen holder

1. Determine the height of the locker. Depending on the height, it may be possible to use two stackable Locker Solutions.

2. On the first day of school, bring the locker organizers. Install the tools before loading the books in the locker.

3. Finish the locker by adding personal touches, such as a magnetic mirror, basket, and pen holder.

Toys

Kids are pros at accumulating stuff. It's not their fault—think of all the toys that are heaped on them by family and friends on birthdays, at Christmas, when Grandma and Grandpa visit, and through any other convenient excuse. And, like adults, once kids have something—especially stuffed animals—they're reluctant to part with it. Here are some projects to help your kids sort through their stuff, store it neatly, and even learn to give some of it away.

Organizing Purses

Little girls and big girls alike love their purses. My daughter started carrying a handbag at age two and eventually gathered a good-sized collection. Storing all those bags is another story.

 TOTAL TIME:
10 to 20 minutes

● **DEGREE OF DIFFICULTY:**
easy

TOOLS:
Adhesive hooks, belt hanger, or wall-mounted hooks.

1. Use any of the recommended tools to neatly organize purses.

2. When using hooks, place them at the level that is easily accessible for your child.

3. Belt hangers are another good solution, but if you use them, balance the purses on both ends of the hanger; otherwise, it will tilt.

Organizing Jewelry

Learning to take care of your valuables is a lesson that can never be learned too young, even if your treasures are made of plastic.

 TOTAL TIME:
20 to 45 minutes
(depending on the number of gems)

● **DEGREE OF DIFFICULTY:**
easy

λ **TOOLS:**
child's jewelry box.

1. Purchase an inexpensive child's jewelry box.

2. Organize the jewelry inside the box, by putting the rings and other items in their designated slots.

3. For those girls with a lot of Bling Bling, purchase additional boxes to accommodate all the gold!

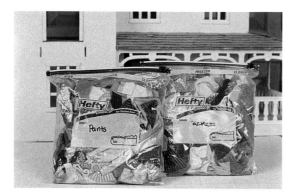

Organizing Dolls

Dolls fall into three categories: baby dolls, Barbie-size dolls, and collectible dolls. Collectible dolls are generally displayed on bookcases or shelving, out of immediate reach. Baby dolls and Barbie dolls, coupled with their clothing, accessories, and miscellaneous other gear, can take over a room.

Girls usually play on the floor with their dolls. Storing dolls in containers under the bed is a perfect, convenient solution. If you have a trundle bed occupying the space under the bed, store the dolls on shelves or in a closet instead.

 TOTAL TIME:
2 to 4 hours (depending on the number of dolls)

● **DEGREE OF DIFFICULTY:**
easy

λ **TOOLS:**
clear plastic containers; large, deep container, rattan basket, or wicker trunk; Ziploc bags, stackable plastic underbed drawers; and portable craft organizer

1. Separate the two types of dolls, clothing, and gear into one pile for baby dolls and accessories and another pile of Barbie dolls and accessories.

2. Separate the baby doll clothing into piles of pants, short dresses, long dresses, tops, skirts, shoes, and other clothing items. Choose a plastic container for each category of clothing that is large enough to hold the items in each pile. Depending on the magnitude of the pile, items may require two or more containers.

3. Label each container with its contents, such as baby doll clothes, baby food, and baby blankets.

4. Place the baby dolls in a large, deep container, rattan basket, or wicker trunk. Store them upright if possible.

5. Separate the Barbie clothing into piles of pants, short dresses, long dresses, tops, skirts, and shoes.

6. Store the Barbie clothes in Ziploc bags. Put each pile of like clothing in a bag and label it.

7. Place the Ziploc bags of Barbie clothes inside a stackable plastic underbed drawer, under the bed.

8. Place the Barbie dolls inside the underbed drawers, as well.

9. Store Barbie shoes, boots, and miscellaneous small objects in the portable craft organizer.

STUFFED ANIMALS

Kids love stuffed animals and cannot part with them. Parents buy them and cannot wait to get rid of them. This is a vicious cycle, and the worst part is, what do you do with them?

Kids need to be weaned from stuffed animals like being weaned from a bottle. It is a slow progression. Parents should *never* take it upon themselves to get rid of any of their children's belongings without consulting them first. Think how you would feel if you came home from work and your "stuff" was gone. A gift is a gift, and your children's toys are their property.

After twelve years of teaching seminars on organization, I have heard many people talk about their baseball cards, dolls, toys, and stuffed animals that were given away without their consent. It has different emotional effects on different people, but the hurt is still there. Parents can keep this hurt from happening by respecting their children's property.

Consult your child when it is time to do some spring cleaning. Tell them that the two of you are going to clean his or her room and give away old toys to charity. Your child will enjoy the process, and it will give you some quality time to spend together.

When you meet with resistance in regard to giving away specific toys, suggest placing items that aren't used often in a storage container that the two of you can revisit in six months. This way, those items will be removed, clearing space in the room, but they won't be gone forever. Do not forget to note the six-month date on the calendar. If your child asks for something stored, thank goodness, you will still have it.

ORGANIZING STUFFED ANIMALS

Stuffed animals "hang out," collecting dust. Here's how to store them dust-free.

TOTAL TIME:
15 minutes to hours (depending on how many critters are hanging out in your house)

DEGREE OF DIFFICULTY:
easy

TOOLS:
plastic storage containers, jumbo stackable storage drawers, and under-the-bed containers

1. Cut down on the dust mites by storing stuffed animals in plastic storage containers.

2. Keep higher-use animals in stackable drawers for easy access.

3. Store Beanie Babies in under-the-bed containers.

Electronic Video Toys

Whether it is PlayStation or Nintendo, the cables, games, and controls of electronic video toys can take over a room. Consider purchasing a game-station holder to keep these items together in one place.

I LOVE MY HOME OFFICE! THERE'S PLENTY OF ROOM
FOR WORK AND STORAGE, AND IT ALL
FITS ON ONE WALL.

Chapter 13

Home Offices

In my opinion, the most important room in a house today is the home office. While a home office can be its own room, it can also be part of another room, such as a guest room, it can take up a portion of the kitchen, or it can be anything in between. Home offices have become a staple in our lives since computers became fixtures in our homes. But there's still a paper trail. Fax machines producing paper, automatic draft capture coming at you faster than you can deposit a check, and the oodles of junk mail that flood the mailbox on a daily basis seem to conspire to have most people buried.

THE PAPER PROBLEM

It is not hard to believe that home offices and all that goes with them have created the number one organizing problem across the board: paper. The paper problem touches everyone, from stay-at-home moms to executives. Paper is an evil that multiplies faster than bunny rabbits. Hopping over the piles has become a common habit, and no matter what is done to eliminate the clutter, it's back in the morning like a bad case of dandruff! Paper is swallowing up our homes and offices, not to mention what it is doing to our trees! Intervention is needed now!

If your papers are out of control, the reason why is simple: You do not have a working file system. If you did, you could locate any document in less than five seconds. The second problem is the approach. Most people go to the stacks and piles of papers and begin by trying to put it into some type of order. This is incorrect. I like to refer to the state of paper shuffling as purgatory. You are doing nothing but treading water, never getting anywhere.

In order to overcome this state, you must follow the steps in this chapter exactly in the order that I have provided them for you. Do not try to skip a step or go another way. If "your way" still leaves you looking and searching for items, then it is time to change "your ways."

You can solve the paper problem by following the system laid out for you here. I like to refer to the system as a cake walk. It is so simple, you'll wonder why it escaped you all of these years. The best part, once everything is in place, is that maintaining it is a breeze with some good established work habits. The 30-Second Rule (putting things away as soon as you are finished using them) will be your salvation in keeping yourself on top of the paper heap.

Begin by thinking of paper as a streamlining system. It has a beginning, middle, and end. The paper has to move through each area until it reaches its final destination. You must create a flow where papers can easily move through, be dealt with, and reach their final resting spot. My system for organizing paperwork has four prongs. What this means is there are four specific parts that work together, making your paper flow easily and helping you stay on top of the paper chase. Each prong handles a specific area: mail and everyday papers, hard-copy papers, tax-receipt papers, and files in the computer.

Before diving into the mechanics, answer these ten questions:

1. Do you open your mail every day?
2. Do you balance your checkbook?
3. Do you own a paper shredder?
4. Do you spend time searching for documents on the computer?
5. Do you lose or misplace important papers?
6. Do you have stacks of papers on your floor and/or desk?
7. Do you lose receipts?
8. Do you keep your tax receipts in a shoe box, bag, or everywhere?
9. Do you pay late fees on bills?
10. Do you want to get control of your paper?

If you answered "no" to questions 1 through 3 and "yes" to questions 4 through 10, your organizing prayers are about to be answered. Remember that anything worth having is worth waiting for. It will take time to go through the process. Give yourself this gift, and you will find sweet success.

ORGANIZING YOUR OFFICE

Where does the all that paper come from? The answer: not the trees! The bulk of it comes from the mail. Knowing that the mail is the source of the problem, you must begin by treating the source. Think of it as a medical condition. When you go to the doctor, do you want him to treat the cause or the effect of your illness? The cause is the right answer. Now, knowing that the cause of your paper problems stems from the mail, you must start there, beginning with the way you handle your mail.

Mail must be opened six days a week. If your office is closed on Saturdays, open the mail first thing Monday morning. Many people who have attended my seminars over the years have stated they get too much mail to open each day. My response is that if you do not open the mail today, there will be twice as much to open tomorrow. Putting off opening the mail will turn a small task into a monumental task the more you delay the process. What once could be done in five to fifteen minutes could take one to two hours. It is much easier to find fifteen available minutes in your day than to two hours. The psychological aspect comes into play, too. By procrastinating, you have changed a fairly simple task into a huge job, and you begin to dread the work ahead.

PRONG I:
MAIL AND EVERYDAY PAPERS

TOTAL TIME:
30 to 45 minutes

DEGREE OF DIFFICULTY:
easy

TOOLS:
recycle bin, paper shredder, Post-it Notes (in any color *but* white), hanging file folders with plastic tabs, desktop caddy, $^1/_3$-cut hanging files, letter or legal size, $^1/_3$-cut file folders, letter or legal size

1. Open the mail every day. Do this over the recycling bin.

2. As you open your mail, treat it as a revolving door in a department store. The minute it arrives, look

through it, open it, and throw out everything that does not belong. For example, think of the perforated advertisements on return envelopes. Look at them when you open an envelope. If you do not want the ads, tear them off and toss them immediately. And toss any ads and materials that were also in the mail that you are not interested in reading. When I say "toss," what I really mean is "recycle."

3. Using Post-it Notes, sort the mail into piles of like items. Write on the Post-it the name of the main heading and the name of the file folder in which you will file the paper. Example: Bills (main heading) 1st of month (file folder).

The reason I have you sort papers and put Post-it Notes on them is very important. The Post-it serves as a flag. You will be making many piles of like papers. Post-it Notes stand out visually, making the piles easy to identify and keeping you from having to constantly re-read what is in each of the piles.

And here's a bonus: Because the piles are flagged with Post-it Notes, when it is time to prepare the labels (later on in steps 7 and 8), it is a breeze to identify the piles. As you stand over each pile, it is only necessary to print what is on the Post-its, without having to read any of the papers for information. This makes the labeling process extremely quick.

Beverly Hills Top Tip

This one's urgent! Purchase a paper shredder. Shred immediately any documents or offers of credit you do not want or need. June 2001 statistics report: The number of consumers who contacted Trans Union's Fraud Victim Assistance Department skyrocketed from 35,000 in 1992 to more than 1 million in 2000. You cannot afford not to shred!

4. The most frequently used main headings for mail and everyday paper hanging files are: Banking, Bills, Catalogs, Coupons, Credit Cards, Filing, Pending, Tax Receipts, and To Do. These are most likely the categories you'll be writing on your Post-it Notes.

Here's the types of mail that falls within each of those categories:

- Banking: Holds deposit slips and ATM receipts, and temporarily holds bank statements before reconciling.

- Bills: Holds bills, stamps, and return address labels.

- Catalogs: Holds pages from catalogs with items you may consider ordering.

- Credit Cards: Holds credit-card receipts for reconciling credit card statements. (We'll talk more about reconciling credit card statements later on page 133.)

- Filing: Holds new papers that need a file and papers that need to be returned to files.

- Pending: Holds items that need to be followed up on.

- Tax Receipts: Holds tax receipts before they're filed in Prong III (We'll talk more about what to do with these at the next stage on page 132).

- To Do: So you won't forget what "To Do."

You may have other main headings, too. The ones listed above are standard. They can be used in both business and personal situations. Others may include your children's school, to read, and so on.

5. Purchase a desktop caddy. This is a small box that holds hanging files that you keep right on your desktop. I have a new name for the desktop caddy. It is O'Hare Airport. Why? O'Hare is the largest layover airport in the United States. What flies into O'Hare is on a temporary layover on its way out to its final destination. Your caddy is your layover for the everyday workings of your life. The mail that flies in will be held there until it is time to move on. Meanwhile, it will be safe, secure, and upright.

Be sure to purchase a caddy that has sides. If you do not, you will risk the chance of losing papers because they may slip out of the open sides.

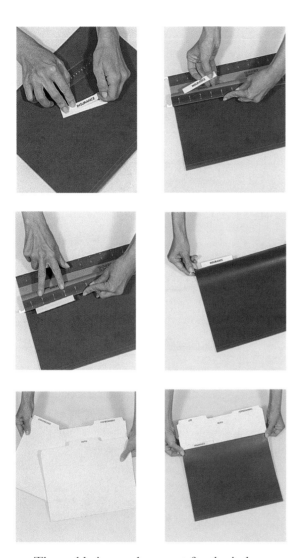

I can't stress often enough how important it is to use a labeler. Make sure you use one to label your files. Did you ever see a newspaper or book that was handwritten? Even when you print in the neatest lettering you possibly can, there are variations in it. Nothing looks cleaner than typeset. Labelers give us a clean, easy-to-read, organized look. Nothing will be able to replace it, and remember: Organization is visual.

Beverly Hills Top Tip

I can't stress often enough how important it is to use a labeler. Make sure you use one to label your files. Did you ever see a newspaper or book that was handwritten? Even when you print in the neatest lettering you possibly can, there are variations in it. Nothing looks cleaner than typeset. Labelers give us a clean, easy-to-read, organized look. Nothing will be able to replace it, and remember: Organization is visual.

The caddy is a replacement for the in box on desks in offices. Remember to think "upright." No more shuffling through stacks of paper lying in trays or piles. The caddy brings the entire stash of day-to-day papers upright, giving you a bird's-eye view of all your daily business. For those people who have an outside office at which other individuals are dropping off papers, prepare a caddy specifically for those papers. You can label it with the name of the person who is doing the delivery. (We'll talk

more about creating files in Prong II, beginning on page 129.)

Also purchase 1/3-cut letter or legal size hanging files and file folders. They must include the three positions (left, middle, and right).

6. Prepare the hanging files and file folders for the caddy. Once you've sorted through your pile of mail, make a file folder for each of the main categories by filling in the cards in the plastic tabs that are included in the box of hanging files.

7. Use a labeler to print labels for the main headings and the file folders. Place the main heading labels directly onto the white insert papers that go inside the plastic 1/3-cut tabs (see photo on page at left).

8. Attach the 1/3-cut tabs to the hanging files. There are many slits on the hanging files, but you are *not* going to use all of them as you may have done in the past. Instead, you are going to pick a side, either the right or left side of the hanging file, skip one slit, and place all of the tabs into the second slit from the end (see photo, above).

Remember the old card catalog index that was used before libraries became computerized? You pulled open a drawer, and all the cards were alphabetized. When the library needed to add a card, they simply dropped it in the correct order in the drawer. All you had to do was let your fingers do the walking. This is exactly how your files will be in Prongs I, II, and III of the working file system. No more readjusting tabs when you get a new main heading. The aggravation is over!

9. Drop the main heading hanging files into the caddy alphabetically.

10. Print out the file folder labels. If there is more than one file folder under a main heading, as you print the labels for those folders, alphabetize the labels by laying them down on your work surface. When it is time to attach the labels to the file folders, you have already pre-alphabetized them.

11. Attach the file folder labels to the file folders. The key is to use the three-position file folders to stagger the files alphabetically. But before you can begin to place the labels on the files, did you choose the left or right side to attach the main heading tabs? Whatever side you chose, *do not* put the first file folder directly behind the tab. One of the mysteries of organizing is the black hole of the file system. If you put the first file folder directly behind the main heading tab, it will be lost. Simply use either of the other two positions available. (Example: If the main heading tab is on the left side, use the middle or right file folder to begin staggering the files.)

Note: If you forget to prepare a file folder or get a new file that belongs with an existing main heading; weave in the new folder alphabetically. For example: Insurance—main heading tab. File folders "Auto" and "Homeowners" are in

positions two and three. The new file is "Earthquake." Weave in "Earthquake" by splitting Auto and Homeowners; insert it in position one. Now the files will read alphabetically.

12. Put the file folders into the main heading hanging files.

13. File papers in the appropriate file folders.

THE FILE CABINET

When I meet with clients to organize their office, the first thing they do is point to all the stacks of papers piled on top of their desks, credenzas, and floors. Frustrated to the point where it is necessary to hire outside intervention, they turn to me and plead for help. My response is, "Where is your filing cabinet?"

As I walk in the direction of the cabinet, my sleeve is tugged upon, and again, I am directed to the piles of papers. Unfortunately, it seems as though I am the bearer of bad news. Before the piles can be addressed, the file cabinet is first in the organizing pecking order.

The reason it is imperative to begin with the file cabinet is because there is a bare-bones organizing skeleton started there. You need to begin with the existing files, no matter how old they may be, and build your system from there. This is a perfect time to spring-clean your files, shredding old documents that are no longer needed and storing others in archival containers.

The two big questions clients always ask at this point are "What to keep?" and "What to toss?" Ask your accountant for his suggestions and guidelines if you are uncertain. If you are in doubt, don't throw it out—prepare a file for it.

Refresh your memory of the very first element we discussed that you need to succeed in organizing:

time. It has taken time to get disorganized, and it will take time to get organized. (See "The First Element: Time" on page 15.) It is of the utmost importance that you follow these guidelines.

Organizing one full file drawer working with me can take approximately four or five hours. How long is it going to take you? Answer: Longer! Play it smart, take out only one or two files at a time. If you follow the plan, working fifteen to twenty minutes at a time, four to five times a day, you can have one full file drawer completely organized within one week, and it will feel like you did nothing. But if you try doing too much, you risk becoming overwhelmed and quitting.

Prong II of the system is for your hard-copy papers. These items could include insurance polices, personal documents, frequent flyer information, and warranties. This is not the place you will store your income tax receipts, but it is the place you will file copies of your tax returns.

As you go through these steps, one thing may be conspicuously absent: I do not believe in color coding. First, it is a big job to organize by color, and second, it is harder to keep it up that way. Running out of a particular color and temporarily using another color in its place is the beginning of the decline. By following the steps of the system outlined for you, color coding is not necessary.

On the other hand, you can use a color file folder in certain situations. If there is a file you constantly go to everyday, you may want to purchase red file folders for those papers. That way, when you open the file drawer, your eyes are immediately drawn to the red files.

Remember, this system is about finding your papers when you need them. It is not about conserving on the number of file folders and hanging files. Water down the system as far as you need to, in order to find a paper when you need it. There are many single sheets of paper out there drifting around your office. Prepare a file for the "one" piece of paper; that way, when you need to put your hand on it, it will be there waiting for you. If you prefer, prepare a "Miscellaneous" main heading and store them in file folders there.

The fun part begins after the file cabinets are in working order. Hang in there, there is a surprise ending!

PRONG II: HARD-COPY PAPERS

TOTAL TIME:
6+ hours (per full file drawer)

DEGREE OF DIFFICULTY:
easy to moderate

TOOLS:
Post-it Notes (any color but white), $1/3$-cut letter- or legal-size hanging files (choose one color with three positions for the tabs: left, middle, and right), $1/3$ cut hanging folders, letter or legal size, $1/3$ cut file folders, letter or legal size, filing cabinet, and plastic containers (for long-term paper storage)

1. Go to the file cabinet and pull out one or two files. (If you do not have a file cabinet, go to the box or bag where the paperwork is being stored and follow the same steps.)

2. Using Post-it Notes, sort the paper into piles of like items. Write on the Post-its the name of the main heading and the name of the file sub-folder the papers will be found under. Example: Insurance (main heading), auto, homeowner, life (file sub-folders). (See the photo on page 127.)

3. Purchase $1/3$-cut letter- or legal-size hanging files and file folders, depending on the size of your cabinet. The box of file folders must include the

Note: By following What You'll Need to Succeed (see page 15), organizing four file drawers will take approximately four weeks to complete.

Surprise ending: Once all the file drawers are organized, it is time to hit the piles on the desk, credenza, and floor. This is when the miracle takes place. Literally 75 to 85 percent of all the paper lying around gets filed. It is the one time you will actually drop fifty pounds (of paper) in a day. For the remaining papers, simply make Post-its for them and follow the preceding steps. It is a cake walk!

three positions (left, middle, and right). The three positions allow you to stagger the file folder alphabetically under the main headings.

4 Use a labeler to print labels for the main headings and the file folders. Place the main-heading labels directly onto the white insert paper that goes inside the plastic ⅓-cut tabs. (See photo, Prong I, Step 7, page 127.)

5. Follow Steps 8 to 12 in Prong I: Mail and Everyday Papers (see pages 127 and 128).

6. During the process, you may trigger your memory and need to prepare a file for a paper that is "out there somewhere." Prepare the main heading and file folders for those papers. When you do come across them at a later date, they will have a home.

More Filing Tips

● Warranties are usually kept together in a big lump. Organize warranties by making a main heading, Warranties. Prepare file folders for each category: appliances (large), appliances (small), computer/ printer, electronics, miscellaneous, telephone/fax, TV/VCR/DVD, stereo equipment, and toys. This way, when you need to get your hands on a warranty, it will be at your fingertips.

● One hanging file will hold one full file folder or up to four slim folders. When a hanging file is overstuffed, another mystical thing happens: growth. The files begin to grow upward, and while opening and closing the cabinet, the edges become worn. Solve this problem by simply using additional hanging files. Spill the file folders over to another hanging file or files.

• Here's how to review your files without opening a drawer. Prepare file drawer sheets for each drawer. Write down each main heading tab and the names of each file under each category. Example:

DRAWER ONE

ADDRESS/PHONE BOOK:
- Address book
- Employee phone numbers

BEACH

BIRTHDAY:
- Birthday ideas

CAMPS

COOKING:
- Catering

- Cooking classes

• When files are being shared by two or more people, there may be discrepancies in the names of the files. One of the people must be the mastermind of the files. This is your system, and to get your hands on a piece of paper quickly, it must be organized by your own thought process. However, when more than one person shares a system, prepare the sheets as stated above but make separate columns for each person so they, too, can locate the files they are looking for quickly. For example:

Linda	Chase
• Auto Insurance	• Car Insurance

• Assume you have a four-drawer filing cabinet. Two and a half drawers are used for business and one and a half are used for personal papers. To indicate where the business or personal files begin, place a main heading tab in the center of the hanging file to designate the change.

• You can also use center tabs to designate changes within the same category. Example: You have three children. The main heading file is called "children." Place a center tab in the center of the first hanging file with one of the children's names; fill those hanging files with their papers. The next hanging file will have the second child's name in the center, and so on.

Older files that need to be kept permanently can be stored in a plastic container, freeing up file drawer space. Use plastic rather than cardboard boxes, especially if you plan on stacking them while in storage. Cardboard boxes can collapse with the weight of other boxes, and they are not safe from rodents or water.

Prong III: Tax Receipts

The third prong of the system is for your tax-deductible receipts. Organize the tax receipts exactly as you have organized the caddy and hard-copy files. The only difference is your system will be stored inside a file crate.

A crate is used for one simple reason: It is portable. You can accumulate receipts 365 days a year, and the idea of being strapped to a file cabinet all year to do your filing is an overwhelming thought. The crate allows you to file whenever, wherever, at your own convenience.

TOTAL TIME:
3 to 8 hours
(depending upon the current order of receipts)

DEGREE OF DIFFICULTY:
easy

TOOLS:
file crate, Post-it Notes (any color but white), ⅓-cut letter- or legal-size hanging files (choose one color 9- by 12-inch envelopes), and plastic storage container

I. Purchase a file crate.

2. Follow Steps 2 to 5 in Prong II: Hard-Copy Papers (see page 129). Create main headings and file folders for each tax-deductible group. Example: Auto (main heading) and car payment, DMV, gasoline, insurance, repair and maintenance (file folders).

Note: It is not necessary to date the file folders. They will be emptied and reused every year. FYI, I have used the same tax-receipt system for twelve years.

3. File receipts once a week or as necessary.

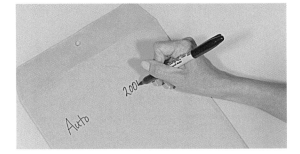

4. At the beginning of the new year, tally the receipts for each category.

5. Record a list of the tax-deductible items and the tallied amounts. Excel is a great program to use for this.

6. Place tallied receipts in 9" × 12" envelopes; use one or two envelopes per main heading. Keep the receipts together yet separated in the large envelopes, by either stapling or putting the receipts in smaller envelopes inside the larger one.

7. Write on the outside of each envelope what it contains, such as Auto 2005, car payments, gasoline, insurance, for example.

8. Store the envelopes in a plastic storage container and label the outside. (Example: 2005 Tax Receipts.)

9. Once the file folders are empty, it is time to start using them again.

Beverly Hills Top Tip

Charitable donations can be used as a tax deduction. It is best, however, to locate a charity that places a value on your contribution for you. This eliminates the guesswork for you and lowers the risk of an audit.

RECONCILING CREDIT CARD STATEMENTS

It is just as important to reconcile your credit card statements as it is your bank statements. Besides staying on top of errors, it is a great way to maximize your tax deductions. Often credit cards are used for business expenses. These expenses can be overlooked when it's tax time if they are not organized.

 TOTAL TIME:
20 to 30 minutes

● **DEGREE OF DIFFICULTY:**
easy

TOOLS:
"Credit Card" main hanging file folder in desktop caddy and $1/3$-cut letter or legal size folders (choose one color with three positions: left, middle, and right

1. Keep a separate file for each credit card in your desktop caddy, in the main hanging file labeled "Credit Cards." (See "Prong I: Mail and Everyday Papers" on page 125.)

2. File charge receipts in the folder on a regular basis to keep from losing or misplacing the receipts.

3. When each statement arrives, match up the charge receipts to the items on the statement. You're checking to make sure that everything was charged to your account correctly. At the same time, evaluate each charge to see if it is tax-deductible or not.

4. Shred receipts that are not tax-deductible.

5. Staple receipts that are tax-deductible to the back of the statement.

6. Code each lined item down the margin. Example: Mobile (code G—for gas).

7. When you've checked each charge on the statement, store the statement in the tax receipts crate under the main hanging file labeled "Credit Cards." (See "Prong III: Tax Receipts" on opposite.)

8. When preparing for taxes, add up all the codes (example: "G") and get the grand total for gasoline, and so on.

PRONG IV: FILES IN THE COMPUTER

Organizing files in the computer is exactly the same as organizing papers. The computer files need to be saved in a main heading file. In my opinion, this is where Bill Gates made a mistake with Windows. Windows displays a file folder as the symbol for saving documents. In actuality, the symbol should have been a hanging file with a $1/3$-cut tab. People become confused, and instead of saving their work as they should, they save individual files. Imagine how big your file cabinet would be if you did not have your papers grouped into main headings. Further, by following the steps in Prong IV, it will cut back on the time you spend searching for documents.

 TOTAL TIME:
1+ hour
(depending on the number of files saved)

● **DEGREE OF DIFFICULTY:**
easy, but tedious

TOOLS:
none required

1. Go to My Documents on your computer.

2. Open a saved file.

3. Click on File.

4. Click on Save As.

5. Click on the folder with an asterisk, New Folder.

6. Create a name for the new folder (main heading name) that will be the place you look for your document. Example: New folder "Correspondence." Saved letters will be placed there.

7. Click OK.

8. Check file name and rename if desired.

9. Click Save.

10. Go back to My Documents and delete the single file.

THE DREADED CHECKBOOK

Offices are generally a place we go to work for the purpose of earning money. It is amazing to me that after working hard to earn a living, most people never reconcile their checkbooks. As a matter of fact, I am comfortable with stating that I believe at least 75 percent of Americans under the age of sixty-five do not balance their checkbooks.

What does this mean? First, banks make mistakes. This is why you are given a statement each month to review. Second, if mistakes have been made, no doubt you have lost money.

I can say this because I have had first-hand experience with balancing checkbooks for more than fifteen years. Further, in every seminar I have conducted, I ask the audience to answer two questions: 1. Do you balance your checkbooks? And 2. How many of those who do balance have found mistakes the bank has made? The answers are staggering: 75 percent answer "no" to question 1 and 100 percent (of people who actually do balance their checkbooks) answer "yes" to question #2.

It is time to organize your money, too. Follow my 12-Step Program to balance your checkbook as outlined here and take back control of your money.

BALANCING YOUR CHECKBOOK

 TOTAL TIME:
30 minutes+
(depending on the number of checks written)

●●● **DEGREE OF DIFFICULTY:**
easy to difficult
(depending on your ease with mathematics)

TOOLS:
calculator

1. Go back two statements.

2. Check off all cleared checks, deposits, debits, and ATM transactions.

3. Place a circle in the columns in which checks, deposits, debits, and ATM transactions are outstanding (the ones that have not cleared the bank).

4. On your current statement, check off all cleared checks, deposits, debits, and ATM transactions.

5. Place a circle in the columns in which checks, deposits, debits, and ATM transactions are outstanding (the ones that have not cleared the bank).

6. Find your balance on the current statement. Write it down in the appropriate place on the back of the statement.

7. Find any bank charges, and write them down in your checkbook near the date posted; check them off.

8. Go back and write down all circled checks, debits, and ATM transaction amounts on the back of the statement, and label them "List of outstanding checks."

9. Balance from the last check that cleared the bank. If there are any deposits made prior to the last check that cleared, write them down under "Deposits not shown" on the statement and circle it in the checkbook.

10. Take the ending balance, add the deposits, and subtract the outstanding checks to get your balance.

11. In your ledger, write down the balance across from the last check that cleared.

12. Continue to add deposits and subtract checks written from this balance to find your current balance.

CALENDARS

Calendars are lifelines to our every waking moment. When life gets too busy, a calendar that "works" can be the only thing that keeps our lives sane. I suggest that busy people keep a large wall or desk calendar that has a monthly overview with day boxes that measure about 2" square. The purpose for the large squares is for visibility and room to write.

Busy moms usually have a team of kids to co-ordinate. Use a different color of marker to code each child's activities. Then, each child can easily check the calendar themselves to see what's on their day's agenda, giving Mom a little break.

COMPUTERIZED ADDRESS BOOKS AND MORE

My favorite way to keep data organized is with a Palm system. Check out the latest products on the market. You will be amazed at the endless possibilities.

A Palm Pilot can organize and balance your personal, professional, and/or academic life. Features include a built-in calendar, contact lists, memo pad, to do list, and advanced calculator, of which can be transferred with a touch of a button to your main computer, because the Palm Pilot is synchronized with Microsoft Outlook and the Palm desktop.

More elaborate systems combine a mobile phone and Palm with wireless communication, including reading and writing emails, text messaging, web browsing, and a digital camera. You are able to check your calendar while talking on the phone, dial calls from your contact list, and take a picture and email it to a friend, because the entire system is integrated. There is a built-in speaker phone, caller ID, and picture ID. Dial anyone from your address book by typing in their name or initials.

Saving time is saving money. Consider using a computerized system like this one to cut down on paper and improve efficiency.

Microsoft Outlook is yet another way to organize your address book and coordinate appointments. There are also programs specifically made to do the same task.

Whatever program you choose, mark your calendar 6 months from completing the entries with a reminder to update the data.

HERE I AM AFTER ANOTHER JOB WELL DONE!
LOOK AT ALL THIS WELL-ORGANIZED ATTIC STORAGE.
YOU CAN DO THIS, TOO!

Chapter 14

Attics, Basements, and Garages

Attics, basements, and garages seem to be the "dump-all" places for objects when they no longer have a use in the house. If this describes your house, do not feel alone! Just take a drive on a Sunday afternoon and peek inside other people's open garage doors. There is no doubt that you will see stacks and piles of clutter. Sometimes there's so much clutter, there is not even room for a car.

Why all the mess? There is a simple answer to this question. Most attics, basements, and garages do not have proper shelving and cabinets. Even if they do,

the placement of all those treasured objects is all wrong. They're shoved, stuffed, crammed, boxed, or bagged, resulting in a cluttered nightmare. So how do you untangle the mess and start fresh? Let's take it one piece at a time.

CREATING CUSTOM STORAGE

Designing custom storage for your attic, basement and garage is a great help. It upgrades your home, adding value and convenience. Follow these two steps for creating a design.

1. Measure the interior of the room—ceiling height, width, and depth. Using graph paper, plot the measurements to scale to get an overview of the room. (See the photo on page 59.)

2. The next step is to plot the placement of the cabinets and/or shelving on the overview. Custom sizes cost more, so start by doing your homework. Choose your products and get the dimensions of the pieces you are interested in. For example, ClosetMaid offers cabinets and wire shelving in a variety of sizes. The overview will allow you to view the space in order to make the correct placement and size choices. Without taking the time to plan ahead, you risk making costly mistakes.

Beverly Hills Top Tip

This one's essential, but it's easy to overlook: Before doing any type of remodeling or construction work on your home, be sure to check with your city building and planning department.

THE ATTIC

Attics generally have sloped ceilings, and they often do not have true floors; instead, they have ceiling joists. But even taking these factors into consideration, with the help of tools, attics can be transformed into useable storage space. This can possibly save you money by allowing you to consolidate the stuff from an outside storage unit with the items in the attic.

Public storage facilities charge monthly rates that can add up to a large sum of money on an annual basis. (We'll talk more about this in Chapter 15.) What are you spending annually in rental fees? If the cost is more than $500 year, it is worth at least considering making over the attic area. Yes, you'll need an outlay of money up front to transform the attic, but as the years pass, you will be saving a small fortune in rent.

If you do not have an attic in your house, is your garage roof pitched? How tall is the highest point of the pitch? The highest point may be tall enough for standing room. Transforming the space above the garage ceiling into a usable attic room can provide much-needed storage. Some garages have open ceilings, in which case it will be necessary to cover the ceiling, adding to the out-of-pocket expense. However, a sturdy floor that can hold the weight of the storage will take you a long way.

Depending on how much you are willing to invest in the space, and what type of storage it will be used for, you may want to add other options such as indoor-outdoor carpeting, fluorescent lighting, and ventilation (always a good idea!). Because garages generally have high ceilings, installing a pull-down ladder is yet another option. I have even had a custom trolley made with a pulley that glides along the sides of my pull-down ladder to help hoist up heavy boxes and containers. (See the photo on opposite page.)

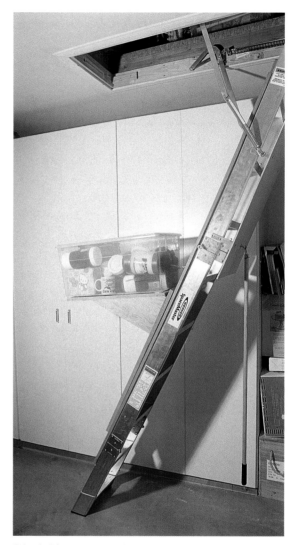

I had this custom trolley made with a pulley to help me haul heavy boxes and containers up the pull-down ladder to the attic. No more fear of falling or dropping boxes!

ORGANIZING ATTICS

TOTAL TIME:
8 to 12 hours (depending on the size of the attic and the size of the mess)

●●● **DEGREE OF DIFFICULTY:**
moderate to difficult

TOOLS:
boxes for donations, clear plastic storage containers, and Rafter Solutions and/or shelving

OPTIONAL TOOLS:
storage cabinets, rolling rod, and garment bags

1. First, you'll need to sort your stuff. This is the trickiest part of organizing an attic that is currently filled. The space is generally cramped, hot, and dirty. If possible, remove boxes from the space to sort elsewhere, otherwise do the best you can by carving out an area to work in.

2. Seriously evaluate your treasures, junk, and "stuff." If it has been up in the attic, long forgotten, it may be time to make a charitable donation. Create giveaway boxes.

3. Sort the "keepers" into piles of like items and place these items into clear plastic storage containers. Label and number each container.

4. Make a handwritten list or create a list on your computer, noting each container's number and contents.

5. Stack the containers into numbered rows, making it easy to locate items when needed, by referring to your list.

6. Use shelving or Rafter Solutions if space permits. Both of these tools are excellent. They allow easier access to storage by allowing removal of containers without a great deal of unstacking and restacking. You can design custom shelving to fit along the lines of the sloped ceiling.

7. If you're storing antiques or sentimental items in your attic, double-protect them by placing them inside plastic storage containers nested inside storage cabinets.

8. If you store clothes on hangers in the attic, purchase a rolling rod and garment bags. The bags protect the clothing from dust, dirt, and insects. Consider using moth repellent to protect clothing even more. Mark your calendar when the moth repellent will need to be replaced.

Beverly Hills Top Tip

It is always a good idea to purchase more containers than you think you will need. This way, if you've underestimated the number you actually need, there is no need to make another store run. Extras can always be returned. However, before making the purchase, ask yourself: Where will these containers ultimately be stored? If your intention is to store them inside a cabinet, take the dimensions of the cabinet shelf space into consideration when buying your containers. You want the containers to fit!

Here's another top tip: Always use clear plastic products. Even with a label on the outside, it is best to be able to view the contents without having to open every container.

Organizing Garages

TOTAL TIME:
8 to 10 hours (depending on the size
of the garage and the size of the mess)

DEGREE OF DIFFICULTY:
moderate

TOOLS:
rafter solutions, clear plastic containers, shelving,
storage cabinets, boxes for donations, clear plastic
stackable drawers,

OPTIONAL TOOLS:
custom closet, bike sport, fishing and garden
racks, parking guide, wall guard, cord wrap, tool
organizers, gardening organizers

*Note: Consider transforming the space above the garage ceiling
into attic storage. (See "Organizing Attics" on page 139.)*

1. Remove the contents of the garage to the
driveway, sorting it into piles of like items, such
as sports gear, tools, gardening supplies, and
cleaning products. (Choose a dry day for this
project!)

2. Once you've finished sorting, store all sorted
items either in clear plastic containers or in
clear plastic stackable drawers. Use the plastic
stackable drawers to store items that require
accessibility, such as holiday items, extension
cords, and backyard lanterns. Use the clear
plastic containers to store items that need to be
packed away. Plastic is the best material for
this type of storage, because it keeps rodents,
insects, and moisture out.

3. Label the outside of each container with a
description of the contents.

4. Put all items that go to charity inside "charity
boxes" that you've marked just for that purpose.

5. Consider coating your garage floor with a two-
part epoxy coating while you have everything
out of it. You'll need to store all your items in
a secure area for twenty-four hours or more.
Coordinate the removal of the contents with
the flooring application, so you'll be prepared.
If you're storing items on a grassy area, use a
tarp to cover the ground and place the stuff on

it, then cover the items removed from the garage with a second tarp.

6. Once the epoxy coating has dried, install the custom garage cabinets, shelving, and/or plastic cabinets. ClosetMaid is an excellent choice for do-it-yourself built-ins and wire shelving.

7. If you want to install a workbench in your garage, it's best to make it kitchen-countertop height: 39" to 40" high. This is a comfortable height for standing, and working. Purchase a stool so you can work sitting or standing as you prefer.

8. If you don't have enough room in the garage for shelving, consider hanging Rafter Solutions. They attach to the rafters in the garage, attic, or basement. Two shelves each hold up to seventy-five pounds of weight. This is an excellent product to use to get items off the floor. It can be used alone or in conjunction with any of the other storage products.

9. If you have a lot of specific sports equipment in your garage, consider buying a sports-specific organizer for them. Racor is the brand name synonymous with sports-equipment organizers. What's your sport? Golf, tennis, biking, skateboarding, fishing, rollerblading, skiing, snowboarding, baseball, hockey, football, basketball—trust me, there is a rack for your racket! Purchase the sports organizers that fit your needs. Get the dimensions of the product and figure out where it will best serve you by consulting your overview, then sketch it in. Install the organizer and load it up.

10. Store cans and bottles inside cabinets, organized the same way you'd organize kitchen cabinets. (Review "Kitchen Cabinets" on page 81.) Complete the finishing touches.

11. Have a cold glass of lemonade, sit back, and admire your handiwork!

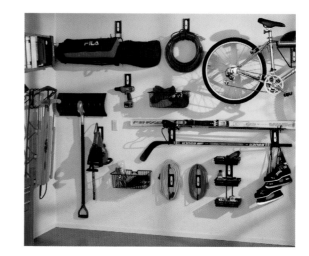

Beverly Hills Top Tip

I highly recommend coating the garage floor for these reasons: A coated floor is easier to clean, makes working in the garage more pleasant, and esthetically, it is gorgeous (for a garage!).

ORGANIZING BASEMENTS

Organizing basements is similar to organizing garages. The biggest problem with this space is where to begin! Basements can be quite large, and they are usually the dumping grounds for the upstairs spillover.

After you've completed the organizing and the area is clean, you might consider doing a room makeover in the basement. You can paint or carpet the floor, put up room dividers, add a drop ceiling, and cover unfinished walls. Convert unused basement space into a gym, media room, wine cellar, game room, laundry room, or play area.

⏱ **TOTAL TIME:**
8 to 12 hours (depending on the size of the basement and the size of the mess)

●● **DEGREE OF DIFFICULTY:**
moderate

⨍ **TOOLS:**
shelving, cabinets, and/or custom closets, clear plastic containers, clear plastic stackable drawers, Rafter Solutions, and boxes for donations

⨍ **OPTIONAL TOOLS:**
custom closets, ClosetMaid ShelfTrack system or cabinets, sports gear organizers, and ceiling hooks

Beverly Hills Top Tip

Rafter Solutions are an inexpensive way to get items off the floor. They have two shelves; each shelf holds up to seventy-five pounds of weight.

1. Determine the type of shelving, cabinets, and custom closets you are going to use. Purchase these items and prepare to install.

2. Purchase the containers that you'll need, such as clear plastic containers and clear plastic stackable drawers, and have them available as you work your way through the "stuff."

3. Clear the area for items in Step 1, so it is ready to receive the containers as they are filled, creating floor space as you work.

4. Start in one corner of the basement and work from that point, sorting items into piles of like items. Seriously evaluate your treasures, junk, and "stuff." If they have been in the basement for a long time, it may be time to make a charitable donation. Create giveaway boxes.

5. Store like items in containers, label, and place them on shelving or inside cabinets.

6. Continue until the entire area has been sorted, organized, and containerized.

Chapter 15

Storage Units

Storage units are a double-edged sword. Technically, storage units should only be used for temporary storing of items due to moving, remodeling, a natural disaster, and so on. They should not be considered a place to dump off clutter that has spun off out of control in the home.

The cost associated with long-term storage is astronomical. Due to the high cost of land, generally a person will pay a minimum of $1,200 a year for storage in metropolitan areas. Economically, consider the value of the items being stored versus the cost of annual storage. Generally, once items are placed in a storage unit, they remain there for years. Let's do the math: $1,200 × 5 years = $6,000.

Do a cost-analysis inventory evaluation of the items you have in storage. Once you have a property value estimate, figure the projected long-term cost of keeping the items stored versus donating the items, taking a tax deduction, and repurchasing items at a later date if needed. When you begin to look at storage from a different viewpoint, it does not make a lot of sense. There are two things that may help you to eliminate long-term storage costs. (See "Attics, Basements, and Garages" on page 136 for storage solutions.)

For those who wish to continue to rent storage space, follow the steps outlined in this chapter to save money by learning how to maximize the square footage and possibly downsize by reconfiguring the space.

ORGANIZING STORAGE UNITS

Follow these instructions if you're moving belongings to a storage unit or if you're organizing an existing unit. Even if an existing unit is currently filled to the ceiling with boxes, you can organize it so that you'll be able to maneuver in the space. If your storage unit is not filled to the ceiling, you will be able to downsize your unit.

TOTAL TIME:
6 to 8 hours (depending on the size of the unit and the amount of belongings)

DEGREE OF DIFFICULTY:
easy to moderate

TOOLS:
plastic storage containers, and shelving

1. I prefer to use plastic storage containers. However, if your items are in cardboard boxes and time does not permit you to transfer everything to plastic storage containers, keep items in labeled boxes and proceed with the following steps. At a later date, try to move items into plastic storage.

2. Measure the ceiling height inside the storage unit and the unit's length. Purchase shelving that will accommodate as much of the vertical space as possible and enough shelving units to fit back to front, leaving about two feet of space between aisles. Think of a library floor plan.

3. Purchase shelving.

4. Empty the storage unit, sorting boxes or containers into piles of like items.

5. Install the shelving in library-aisle fashion, starting by lining one of the side walls with shelving from back to front.

6. Label and number each container or box.

7. Make a handwritten list or use a computer, noting each container or box number with its contents.

Beverly Hills Top Tip

Plastic storage containers keep out moisture, rodents, and insects, and they prevent crushing, a frequent peril when using cardboard boxes.

8. Stack containers or boxes into numbered rows, making it easy to locate items when needed, by referring to your list.

9. Begin a new aisle of shelving approximately two feet across from the first row. Continue with Steps 7 through 9.

10. Continue organizing the unit this way, until all items have been placed on shelves inside the storage unit.

11. Keep a copy of the list of contents in the storage unit and a back-up copy in a file at home.

Chapter 16

Moving

It has been said that moving is one of the three greatest stressors known to man, the other two being death and divorce. Moving is a pain, but it's hardly a stressor compared to the others. Moving can actually be fun when it is well thought out, there is a plan in place, and you organize as you go. I've included moving in this section because when you move, it really involves the whole house!

Moving can be an expensive endeavor, and it can cost more than it should when you are not organized. But moving does not have to cost an arm and a leg. It can be done fairly inexpensively, depending on what lengths you are willing to go, the distance of the move, and the timeline.

In 2003, I moved a three-bedroom house with three baths and a two-car garage into a two bedroom with two baths and no garage for less than $450. How is this possible? Read on….

MOVING OUT

You'll have a much better moving experience if you master the basics of moving before you're right in the midst of it. Use this checklist to get your move underway.

• Give yourself time. Extra time saves money, cutting down on the moving expenses.
• Begin packing immediately.
• Purchase used boxes from a moving company or go to a store that recycles their boxes, such as warehouse stores Smart & Final. S&F has a container that is specifically designed for box disposal. They have small- to medium-size boxes, and best of all, they're *free*. You must be prepared to get up early, before all the good ones are gone.

Beverly Hills Top Tip

When you see other people moving, ask them if you can have their used boxes.

• As you pack up clothing, count your shoes and measure the linear footage of your clothing. (See "Closets" on page 52.) Now you can determine how much space you need in your new closets to accommodate your clothing. If you find you have more clothes than will fit in your new closets, this is a great time to get rid of extra clothes. Why pack and move clothes then give them away after you move in. Give them away now! This is true not just for clothes, but for every item you move. So be prepared to "move in" in advance.

• If any of your furniture needs to be reupholstered, moving time is the time to make those arrangements. If you're moving within the same area, coordinate with your upholsterer to pick up the furniture at your old residence but deliver it to your new residence. This will save you the cost and time of moving those pieces. And some upholsterers pick up and deliver free of charge! Of course, this will not work for you if it is geographically impossible.

• As you are pack and pare down your belongings, if there are items that you don't want to move but are too good to throw away, hold a moving sale. Sales can subsidize the cost of your move. Just before you plan to move, have a yard or garage sale. You can earn money to offset a big part of the moving expenses. Put up large, neon-colored, poster board-sized signs on the Thursday evening before the Saturday morning sale. It's best to use words like "Huge Moving Sale." Don't forget arrows pointing to the direction of the sale. This way, passers-by will take note of the sale coming home from work on Thursday and again as they pass by on Friday. They will not forget about your sale!

• As you pack up your things in boxes, create an inventory list. Write a list with the box number and brief description of contents. Use Excel if you have the program. You can track the whereabouts of boxes if any "fall off the truck." This is a great way to save money if you plan on purchasing moving insurance but not buying too much and don't want to find that you've regretfully purchased too little. It is also great if things do go missing.

• Number each box and mark it with its destination.

• Before you leave your old home, photograph and/or videotape its condition to secure the return of the security deposit or defend yourself against the complaints of a buyer.

• If you are hiring a moving company, check out the movers with the Better Business Bureau. Some movers have hidden costs and tons of complaints. It is best to pay more up front rather than deal with the headaches of damaged goods and added expenses later.

• If you are renting a van to move things yourself, carefully check into rates. U-Haul sometimes has better rates on weekdays. If you intend to use this form of transportation, check out the savings.

MOVING IN

• Save on moving costs by taking occupancy of your new residence one to two weeks prior to vacating your existing property. (This may be too costly or not available to you.) There are two reasons to do this: It gives you the leisure time to move things over yourself bit by bit and begin putting things away as you go. And it can save you a tremendous amount in moving costs. Weigh the cost of occupancy vs. moving costs and convenience.

There is nothing like moving in and spending your first night with 90 percent of your boxes already unpacked and their contents ready to use or enjoy!

• Pick up a change of address form at the post office. Many times, there are coupons for movers and storage companies in these forms. Put in your change of address early with the post office. You will have a better chance of getting all your mail delivered more promptly. Also, if you follow my advice and take occupancy one to two weeks early, you will not lose any residual mail that continues to arrive at your old address.

• Arrange to have your electric, gas, cable, water, and other services connected in your new home the day before you move in. Turn off service at your old address the day after you move out.

• As you move in, note damages in writing prior to moving into a new residence. Going on record with problems early can save you headaches later.

• Checkmark the boxes off the list as you move them in.

PART FOUR

Keepsakes and Holidays

Chapter 17

Magazines and Newspapers

What do people love to save, have no time to read, and are guilt-ridden over if they toss out? Magazines and newspapers, of course!

Getting control of the paper flow is a difficult maneuver for many people. They feel they will miss something if they let an issue go. Therefore, the stacks build, and so does the guilt. Take back your power and stop the paper pressure!

One way to begin is by cutting back on the number of subscriptions you receive. Only accept those issues you have time to read. It's easy to keep up with the news over the Internet or on TV. Consider subscribing to a weekend edition of your local paper instead of subscribing for the entire week.

Once the cutbacks and concessions have been made, it is time to dig into the piles. If you're serious about going through the stacks of magazines and newspapers stored around the house and office, take one or two issues a day to a quiet place to read. Whittle through the mounds this way. When confronted with an enormous pile, some people shut down. It is too overwhelming. (If you feel this way, review "What You'll Need to Succeed," beginning on page 15.)

SAVING MAGAZINES AND NEWSPAPER CLIPPINGS

There are two types of magazines: keepers and cutters. Keepers are magazines that you prefer to keep intact. Cutters are those magazines and newspapers you clip or tear articles out of before throwing the rest away. Here's how I deal with each type.

ORGANIZING KEEPER MAGAZINES

Once you've decided to keep a magazine, it is time to begin creating an index listing for each publication. (Hmmm… are you beginning to reconsider? Maybe you don't need to save it after all!)

⏱ **TOTAL TIME:**
time it takes to read a magazine

● **DEGREE OF DIFFICULTY:**
easy

⚒ **TOOLS:**
3-ring binder, sheet dividers with tabs, notebook paper, and magazine holder

1. Make a list of the subscriptions that are keepers.

2. Prepare a sheet divider tab in your 3-ring binder for each subscription. (Use your labeler.) Example: *Gourmet* magazine.

3. Alphabetize the dividers and put them inside the 3-ring binder.

4. Label the outside of the binder: Recipes, Articles, and so on.

5. Put notebook paper behind each divider.

6. As you go through each magazine, write the month and year of the issue on the top of a new sheet of notebook paper in that magazine's section in the binder. In the margin, write the page number, and in the center of the page, write the article or recipe title. For example, if the May 2005 issue of *Gourmet* just arrived, flip to the "*Gourmet*" divider tab. Write "May 2005" at the top of a clean sheet of paper.

7. While navigating and reading through the issue, write down the page numbers and articles or recipes that interest you on the notebook paper, creating an index.

8. Once you have finished with that issue, there may be room left over on the page. Highlight the month and year so it stands out on the page. When the next month's issue arrives, simply skip a line or two and begin again, writing down your interests, and highlight that month and year.

9. Store issues you've finished reading by subscription in a magazine holder. Label the holder, for example: "*Gourmet* January 2005"

10. When the magazine holder is full, put another label on the holder with the month and year of the last issue, for example: "through November 2005."

11. Store the magazine holders on bookcases or shelving inside closets, depending on how often you think you'll refer to them.

12. Keep the recipe-index binders with your cookbooks. Store article-index binders on bookcases or shelving inside closets, depending on how often you think you'll refer to them.

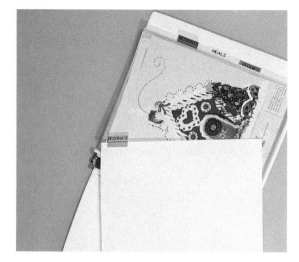

ORGANIZING CUTTER MAGAZINES AND NEWSPAPER CLIPPINGS

Organizing tear sheets and clippings is very similar to the process you used for Keeper Magazines (see page 154). The difference is that instead of writing down an index, you'll slip articles and/or recipes into plastic covers called sheet protectors.

 TOTAL TIME:
1 to 2 minutes (per clipping)

 DEGREE OF DIFFICULTY:
easy

TOOLS:
sheet dividers with tabs, 3-ring binder, and sheet protectors

1. Prepare a sheet divider tab for each area of interest or recipe type, such as Desserts, Pasta, Poultry, and Seafood. Label them with your labeler.

2. Alphabetize the dividers and put them inside the 3-ring binder.

3. Label the outside of the binder, such as Recipes or Articles.

4. Put sheet protectors behind each divider tab.

5. Slip tear sheets and clippings inside the sheet protectors under the appropriate divider tab.

6. Keep recipe binders with your cookbooks. Store article binders on bookcases or shelving inside closets, depending on how often you think you'll use them.

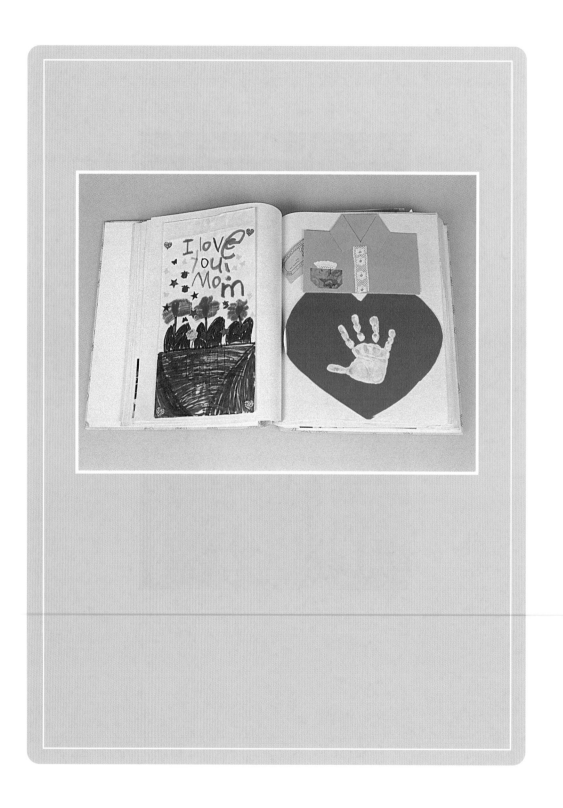

Chapter 18

Mementos

Mementos and keepsakes are those precious items we cannot bear to throw out. However, these sentimental treasures are usually stuffed in bags or packed in boxes and stored away for another day when there will be time to organize and reminisce.

"Another day" is here. The 30-Second Rule applies to mementos, too. When you take the time to put things away neatly as they arrive in your life, the task is small and painless, and not time-consuming. It is only when months pass into years, and photos, newspaper clippings, and various mementos pile up, that the task becomes a monumental project.

Don't concern yourself about the stacks, bags, and boxes right now. Work in the moment, organizing the items that arrive now. As you begin to organize these things, and they start taking shape, little by little you'll begin sorting out the past. Eventually your past will catch up with you!

CREATING SCRAPBOOKS

Scrapbooks are a wonderful way to store mementos. Starting a scrapbook for each family member is a great place to begin. Purchase age-appropriate scrapbooks, because one scrapbook will never be large enough to accommodate the first eighteen years. The different scrapbooks will represent the child's life progression. For adults, when you find a scrapbook you love, purchase plenty of refill pages, and consider buying one or two extra books. This way, you will have two or three extra volumes ready when you need them. You can also place a label on the spine noting the year(s). Keep the scrapbooks on a bookcase or shelf where they can be easily accessible for mounting new keepsakes.

The hobby of scrapbooking is fast becoming a new rage. This craft combines art and mementos, to create a whole new art form. There are clubs and parties at which people meet specifically to "scrapbook" together. Whatever way you prefer to make them, from simple to elaborate, scrapbooks are keepsakes that you will treasure forever.

CREATING HOMEMADE SCRAPBOOKS

 TOTAL TIME:
1 to 3 hours
(depending on the amount of memorabilia)

● **DEGREE OF DIFFICULTY:**
easy and fun!

 TOOLS:
package of 11" × 14" poster board, hole punch, and ribbon, raffia, or string, and mounting squares

I. Purchase tools.

2. Make two holes in each piece of poster board. Be careful to line up the holes exactly.

3. Run a piece of ribbon, raffia, or string through the holes, creating a book.

Beverly Hills Top Tip

Create scrapbooks for greeting cards from birthdays, anniversaries, baby showers, weddings, and holidays. You can even handwrite on the card or on the poster boards a description of the gift that accompanied each card.

---

4. Organize your memorabilia in chronological order, to the best of your ability.

5. Artistically arrange the keepsakes on the poster board.

6. Attach mounting squares to the back of each keepsake and stick the item down on the poster board. Fill the pages with your favorite memories.

7. Decorate the cover of the scrapbook with something special and meaningful, such as an invitation or ribbon box.

ORGANIZING POSTCARDS, LETTERS, AND GREETING CARDS

It is difficult even for me to part with sentimental cards, letters, and postcards. They hold such special memories from holidays gone by, friends, and happy times. Keep these treasured memories organized and in a convenient place where you can add to the collection—in a closet or on a shelf.

 TOTAL TIME:
1 to 2 hours
(depending on the amount of keepsakes)

● **DEGREE OF DIFFICULTY:**
easy

 TOOLS:
File crate or stacking file drawer
and ¹/₃-cut letter-size hanging files

OPTIONAL TOOLS:
¹/₃-cut letter-size file folders

I. Purchase a file crate or stacking file drawer.

2. Using hanging files, create a main heading tab for each family member.

3. If you want to create sub-folders, create separate annual file folders inside each hanging file, designating birthdays, holidays, etc.

4. File each keepsake in the appropriate folder.

Beverly Hills Top Tip

Always put the date on the back of the keepsakes to make filing simple. Then, if the items get misplaced, you will know where to refile them.

Beverly Hills Top Tip

Create a file for photos of other people's kids, family, or friends that will not be included in your family photo album.

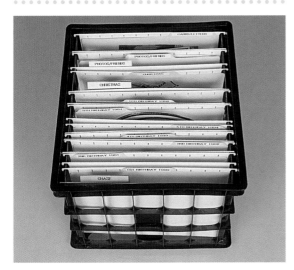

SAFEGUARDING HOME VIDEOS

Many new parents-to-be's first major purchase at the news of pregnancy is a video camera. Everyone becomes a director and filmmaker when a little one arrives. These treasured moments caught on tape can never be replaced. Follow these tips to keep your past safe in the future.

 TOTAL TIME:
5 minutes +
(depending on the length of the recording)

● **DEGREE OF DIFFICULTY:**
easy

 **TOOLS:**
extra blank tapes

1. First, before putting the tape in the machine, attach a label to the cassette. Note the date and special event (if any).

2. Always note the date on tape for backup, in case the label dries up and falls off.

3. Take the tape out of the camera after use to prevent rewinding and accidentally rerecording over the tape.

4. When you've finished recording the tape, make a duplicate tape for backup, and keep it in a fireproof box, a safe-deposit box, or at a relative's home.

5. Keep tapes stored in video or tape holders, or consider burning copies onto DVDs.

Chapter 19

Photo Albums

The most precious things in the world to us are kids, pets, and photo albums. Photo albums keep distant memories at the forefront of our minds as we reminisce about years gone by and walk down memory lane. Keeping these treasures safe, secure, and organized can be a challenge.

Everyone has good intentions to put their photos away in an album, but few of us seem to ever get around to doing it. I compliment those rare and organized individuals who put their photos away immediately after they are developed or printed. More often than not, however, photos stack up, and before we know it, many years pass, leaving our neglected treasures scattered in various places collecting dust—and, of course, unseen by us.

Digital cameras have taken the market by storm, allowing savings on film and processing. But however you keep your digital images, whether they're saved on disk or saved in the computer, printed copies still need to be organized.

ORGANIZING PHOTOS

For a moment, forget about the accumulation of photographs that you have been collecting for years. Yes, they need to find their way into albums, or to simply be stored correctly, but I do not want you to concern yourself with this issue now. Begin by organizing all the new photos you get from the first day they arrive in your life. Follow the steps I have listed below. I have not designated a preparation and organizing time for this project. Work at your own pace, enjoy reminiscing, and take the time you need to protect your memories.

TOOLS:
archival-safe photo albums and protectivesheets, light box, archival negative sleeves, negative binder, fireproof box or safe-deposit box, and photo box

1. Go to a camera store that sells archival-safe photo albums and protective sheets. It is important to use these products because photos will degrade over time if you do not take the proper steps to protect them.

2. If your camera has the capability to stamp the date a photograph was taken right on the picture, I recommend using that feature. Dates are important, especially if your family takes similar trips every year, because you sometimes

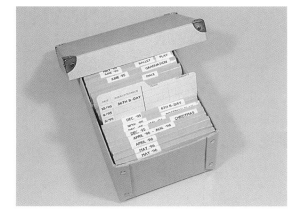

can't tell one year from the next. This is confusing when you try to put the album together in chronological order.

If your camera does not provide a date, make a point to begin labeling each package of photos with the month(s), year, and special event, if any.

3. Separate the negatives from the photos. Using a light box, pull the negatives that match your favorite pictures and place them inside archival negative sleeves. Write on the sleeves pertinent information about the photos, such as the month, year, and event. Place the negatives inside a negative binder and inside a fireproof box or safe-deposit box.

If you don't have a light box, you can make one. Using a glass table or surface, put a lamp under the glass. This works great as a makeshift light box.

By following these steps, you have just insured that you will be able to find a negative for reprinting when needed, and you have stored and protected your negatives apart from your albums. If there is ever a fire or natural disaster, at least you will be able to have prints made from your negatives. All memories will not be lost.

4. Keep the photos inside the photo packages they come in from the developer. Label them with the month, year, and special event if any. Place the photo packages inside a photo box in chronological order.

5. When you are ready to slip the photos into the archival protective sheets, the photos can easily be put in chronologically. Put a label on each sheet, noting the event, place, and date. Photos that are not put inside the new album will be kept inside the photo packages, in the photo boxes.

6. Be careful where you store your photo albums. Varnished bookcases sometimes have vapors that the human nose cannot detect; however, these vapors can destroy pictures over an extended period of time.

OLDER PHOTOS

Photos from the past that have not made it into albums require more time to organize. Do not become overwhelmed. Begin by taking out a few packages or loose photos. Sort the photos into piles by year and then by month. Using Post-it Notes, write the year on the Post-its, and begin sorting.

Once you have compiled a group of photos for any particular year, prepare Post-its for each month. Separate the photos by month. Use the same Post-its as dividers for the groups of pictures. Store the photos in a photo box or boxes until you are certain there are no further pictures for that given year. Then follow the instructions for "Organizing Photos" on page 161.

Do you have any old albums that are the "peel and stick" type? The glue used in this type of album can be damaging to the photographs. I recommend disassembling these old albums and following the same instructions for organizing these photos. (See "Organizing Photos" on page 161.) Again, this is a process that will take time. Don't become overwhelmed. Pace yourself and enjoy the stroll down memory lane.

YOU CAN TUCK A CRAFT OR GIFT-WRAP CENTER
ALMOST ANYWHERE. NEXT TIME, EVERYTHING YOU
NEED WILL BE IN ONE PLACE—AND IN GREAT SHAPE!

Chapter 20

Holiday Time

Do you buy new wrapping paper, bows, and gift or greeting cards every year because you can't remember what you did with the old ones (or they got crushed beneath a pile of other stuff)? Don't let it happen again!

Crafting and gift-wrapping are two favorite pastimes of both adults and children. But finding a place to house all the notions, beads, yarns, and whatnots can be the biggest pain of all. Organizing them is usually an afterthought.

Where do you do your crafting or wrapping? Most people will use a desk, dining room table, or even the floor. Having a special area on which to spread your materials out on and work your magic seems to be only possible in your dreams. A craft or gift-wrap center does not have to be a luxury space only available to the wealthy. I have created these special areas in many nooks and crannies around my clients' homes, including closets, garages, and dining rooms.

CREATING A CRAFT OR GIFT-WRAP CENTER

TOTAL TIME:
4 to 6 hours (depending on space)

 DEGREE OF DIFFICULTY:
easy to moderate

TOOLS:
table, slat board or Peg-Board and hooks, chair or stool, shelving, baskets, craft containers, round clothing rods, rod cup holders, and melamine or lumber 12" to 14" deep

OPTIONAL TOOLS:
wrapping paper station, portable craft organizer, painter's box, 64-drawer craft center, 26-drawer craft center, 16-drawer craft center, stamp camper, craft cases, and craft caddy

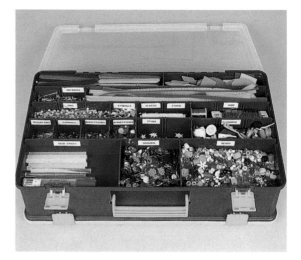

1 Find a place against a wall that is at least 36" wide to station the craft or gift-wrap center.

2. Decide on your work surface height. It can be desktop height (30" tall) or kitchen countertop height (40" tall). My personal preference is a 40" height, allowing for comfort standing or sitting on a stool.

3. Purchase a table for your center or make one. Either way, the end results will be fabulous!

4. After the table has been chosen, purchase the slat or Peg-Board the same width as the table. If you go with the slat board, purchase hooks for scissors, tape, ribbon, etc. Peg-Board can be purchased inexpensively, and you can buy small plastic jars that can hold notions and Peg-Board hooks that can hold pliers, scissors, andother items. Either option works beautifully.

5. Frame either side of the slat board or Peg-Board with piece of melamine or lumber. If space permits, consider purchasing melamine shelving for one or both sides of the table. The pieces that frame the board will hold the clothing rods between them.

6. Install the clothing rods. The rods will hold rolls of wrapping paper, necklaces, bracelets, ornaments, and so on. Use only round rods for rolls of gift wrap.

7. Purchase additional baskets or drawers for extra supplies.

8. Use any number of the optional tools to organize your craft supplies.

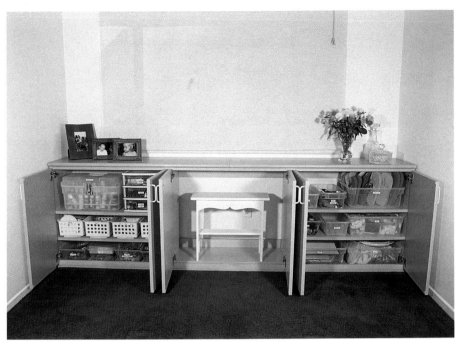

This craft buffet is a wonderful workplace for making crafts, and as you can see, it holds a world of supplies. But when the doors are closed, it's just an attractive piece of furniture, and it can be used as a dinner buffet!

Here's the diagram I used to custom-design my client's craft buffet. See how it fits perfectly beneath the window and uses every inch of available space.

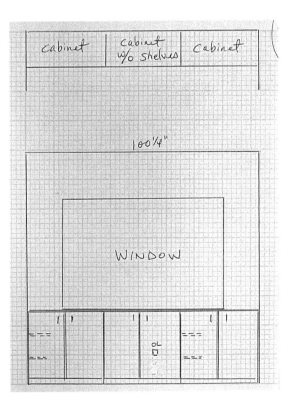

Craft Buffet

Creating space where there appears to be none is my greatest forte. Look at the pictures of this buffet. Before the buffet was designed and installed, the homeowner had her home-based accessories business on the dining room table. Using the dead space under the dining room window, I designed a three-cabinet storage area. The two end cabinets hold the accessories and supplies. The center doubles as a work space and houses a stool when not in use. And the entire countertop can be used as a buffet when needed. Let your imagination run wild. The possibilities are endless. Whether you have a house, apartment, or condo, you have space. Go find it!

HOLIDAY STORAGE

Holidays are a wonderful time to celebrate and decorate your home with the beautiful, sentimental items you have collected over the years. Often, though, many of the treasures are too hard to find and dig out, or are broken due to poor packing and storage. There are many tools made specifically to handle the long year's nap and keep your treasures safe, secure, and organized.

Unfortunately, most of these organizing tools are only available in retail outlets seasonally. Plan ahead and do your shopping early. The following list of holiday organizing tools features my personal favorites. Make sure you stock up this year!

- 12-gallon holiday lights and garland storage box

- 12-gallon ornament storage box

- Light wrap

- Holiday wreath box

- 6-drawer ornament chest with dividers (holds 72 ornaments)

- 3-drawer ornament chest with dividers (holds 48 ornaments)

- Stackable drawers with dividers

- Plastic containers with dividers

- Plastic dinnerware set with dividers (holds an 8-piece holiday place setting)

- Wrapping paper container

- Artificial Christmas tree and accessories container

Getting organized for the holidays may seem like effort now, but think how much stress it will save you, when the whirlwind of "things still to do" is upon you. You'll have that much more time to enjoy yourself and make happy memories!

PART FIVE

Resources

Favorite
Non-Organizing Products

No home is complete unless it is supplied with my three favorite non-organizing products. Organizing is a derivative of housecleaning. And cleaning means having numerous cleaning supplies to handle cleanups and odors. Reducing the number of products you need cuts down on the amount of space you need to store them, and it saves money. All three of these products are miracle workers, and I am happy to recommend them to you.

FOLEX

This is an amazing stain dissolver. Wine, blood, vomit—you name it, it is gone. Spray Folex on carpet, clothing, and furniture, anywhere, and everywhere. This product is best used when the stains are fresh, but I have seen it work on old, set-in stains. Hit the spray trigger and watch the stains disappear before your eyes!

www.folexcompany.com

ODORZOUT

Invented by "Dr. Stink," this odor-eliminating powder will take the stink out of any stench. There's no need to throw out rugs and carpets with pet odors. Sprinkle on this powerful (but animal- and child-friendly) product, and the odors are pulled out of the carpets right down to the matting and floor board. Sprinkle it in litter boxes, trash cans, and diaper pails—anywhere there is an odor. Best of all, Odorzout works even if the odors have been there for years. Odorzout works magic!

www.88stink.com

NO-GO

Do you have someone with four feet living in your house ?

If your answer is yes, No-Go is a must-purchase item. When you want to keep pets off furniture, or stop them from making "messes," spray No-Go on that area. You can't smell it, but they can, and they don't like it. Your pets will stop the behavior without your having to raise your voice or even a newspaper.

www.vetvax.com/housebreakingaids.html

Emergency and Disaster Supplies

Hope for the best, prepare for the worst. This should be everyone's policy when making preparations for emergency and disaster supplies. Somehow along the way, we put off important things in life, in the hope that if we are not prepared, it will not happen to us. Other issues also get in the way of making those important preparations: the outlay of money for things you will only throw away later, you're too busy to think about it, or that you have no place for it if you bought it.

However, very few people could go to sleep and rest comfortably at night knowing that they did not have insurance—auto, health, homeowners', disability, and life. There is a sense of security in knowing that you are covered if the unthinkable happens. When it comes to emergency supplies, we should take the same approach.

Begin to think of emergency and disaster supplies as a form of insurance. Better yet, it's insurance that you actually get something out of whether or not you use it in a time of need. What I mean is, emergency and disaster supplies are the only real insurance we have that we can recycle. Recycle them by using up the bulk of the products you buy and replacing them with new ones as time goes on.

Over the years, I have organized emergency supplies for many families, only to be called back five years later to throw out the old and purchase new products. You need not waste any more! Be prepared in more than one way. After you do your shopping for supplies, make a list of the items you purchased, with the expiration dates and/or the date you purchased the items. This way you will be able to use the supplies and replenish them on a regular basis. Now, with what other insurance can you do that?

Mark your calendar every six to eight weeks, or whatever feels comfortable to you, to check on the rotation of products in your emergency supplies.

BEING PREPARED

Just how many types of emergencies should you be prepared for? Depending on your geographic location, there are a number of possible disasters you should be prepared for, such as earthquakes, extreme cold, heat waves, fire, flood, hurricanes, mudslides, thunderstorms, tidal waves, tornadoes, volcanoes, wildfires, winter storms, and even bombing and nuclear attacks. Find out what natural disasters are most common in your area.

Historically, flooding is the nation's single most common natural disaster. Flooding can happen in every state in the United States. Earthquakes are often thought of as a West Coast phenomenon, yet forty-five states and territories in the United States are at moderate to high risk of earthquakes. That's every region of the country. Not to be the bearer of bad news, but anything is possible. It can even snow in Tucson, Arizona!

Do you have medical release forms prepared for your minor children? God forbid your child is injured and you are not able to be there to make medical decisions. Fill out the necessary medical release forms and give them to the person(s) responsible for the care of your child.

Buying and Storing Supplies

Before purchasing the products you need, figure out where you will store the items, such as in your closet, basement, or garage. The popular thought is to keep these items in large trash cans. I disagree. The last thing you want to do is mix your batteries with your Carnation Instant Milk. Further, your items should not be dumped in a deep can that you cannot get to or transport easily. The best thing to do is purchase a few stackable containers in varying sizes: 8-gallon, 11-gallon, and 13-gallon. Keep your toiletries in the 8-gallon, food in the 11-gallon, and blankets, change of clothing, shoes, and so on. in the 13-gallon. The containers can easily be transported to the trunk or back seat of a car in case of an evacuation emergency.

It is best to stock up on enough emergency supplies to last at least seventy-two hours. Purchase food that stores well without refrigeration, such as:

- Canned meats, fish, soup, macaroni, beans, chili, vegetables, spaghetti, ravioli, fruit, juice, nuts, peanut butter, jelly, pudding, and dried milk

- Nuts, raisins, hard candy, gum

- Turkey or beef jerky

- Staples such as crackers, cereal, rice cakes, snack bars, and dried fruit (Transfer them from their bags or boxes to plastic jars.)

- Baby food
  (if there's a baby in your household)

- Pet food (if there are pets in your household)

Buy foods that are low in sodium so as not to deplete your water supply. Water is critical. Purchase from one to two gallons of water per person per day. In extreme cases, a toilet tank can provide up to seven gallons of water. Do not drink it if chemical disinfectant agents were used.

Other items your home and office emergency kit should have are:

- Can opener

- Vitamins

- Sleeping bags

- Tent

- Rain gear

- Shampoo

- Grill

- Camp stove

- Fuel for cooking
  (charcoal, camp stove fuel, and so on.)

- Plastic plates, cups, knives, forks, and spoons

- Paper towels

- Special tools and supplies (axe, shovel, broom, crescent wrench, screwdriver, pliers, hammer, rope, toys for children)

- Car supplies (see below) these items should be at home, too

Each person also needs one complete change of warm clothing:

- Jacket or coat

- Long pants

- Long-sleeved shirt

- Sturdy shoes

- Hat

- Gloves

- Warm blanket

In case of a biological threat, be prepared to protect your nose, mouth, eyes, and cuts in your skin. Anything that fits snugly over your nose and mouth, including any dense-weave cotton material, can help filter contaminants in an emergency. There are also a variety of face masks readily available in hardware stores that are rated based on how small a particle they can filter in an industrial setting. Worse-case scenario: Use a T-shirt to cover your nose, eyes, and mouth.

Car Supplies

It is very possible that when an emergency strikes, you may be stuck in your car for several hours. Think of all the things you will need for basic comfort and store them in a backpack in the trunk of your car. You can also keep items contained in file crates. Some of those items should be:

- Full tank of gas

- Cash

- Flashlight and extra batteries

- AM radio (to save your car battery)

- Eyeglasses

- First-aid kit (see below)

- Thomas guide or navigation system

- Walking shoes

- Fire extinguisher

- Bottled water

- Energy bars, nuts, or granola

- Thermal foil blankets

- 2-day supply of daily medication

- Personal hygiene items (toothpaste, toothbrush, sanitary supplies, tissue)

- Whistle

- Waterproof matches

- Flares

- Ziploc bags, toilet tissue, newspaper

- Note pad, pen, book, card

First-Aid Kit

First-aid kits should contain the following items:

- Aspirin
- Anti-diarrhea medication
- Laxative
- Scissors
- Tweezers
- Razor blades
- Safety pins
- Band-Aids (all sizes)
- Compresses
- Butterfly bandages
- Gauze pads
- Burn spray
- Smelling salts
- Insect-bite medication
- Rubbing alcohol
- Hydrogen peroxide
- Vaseline
- Antiseptic soap
- Hot and cold packs
- Sunscreen

Supply Shelf Life

Remember, emergency and disaster supplies can be recycled (used up or consumed and replaced). The following list is a helpful guideline for replacing stored foods:

FOOD	MONTHS
Canned	
Meat	18
Poultry	18
Berries	12
Citrus fruit juices	12
Other canned fruit and fruit juices	18
Fish	12
Tomatoes	12
Sauerkraut	12
Other vegetables	18
Cereal products	18
Condensed meat and vegetable soups	12
Cereals and baked goods	
Cereals in metal containers	12
Cereals in original package	4
Uncooked cereal (instant) in metal	24
Uncooked cereal in original package	12
Pancake mix in airtight container	6
Milk	
Evaporated	6
Dry	6

Miscellaneous

Dried fruit in metal containers	12
Instant potatoes	18
Instant coffee, tea, cocoa	18
Bouillon	12
Beverage powders	24
Pasta and white rice	24
Rice mixes	6
Instant breakfasts, liquid, bars	6
Peanut butter	9
Nuts	2
Vegetable oil	3

Sugar and Sweets

Granulated sugar	24
Brown and powdered sugar	4
Hard candy and gum	18
Honey, jelly, syrups	12
Pudding mix in original package	12

Emergency Meal Planning

One of the biggest problems with emergency foods is trying to plan a meal. Before going to the supermarket, make a shopping list based on the sample menu below. (Note that some of these things require water and/or heating, such as oatmeal and hot chocolate. Plan accordingly.)

Breakfast

- Cereal, granola, or instant oatmeal
- Brown sugar
- Canned juice
- Hot chocolate

Lunch

- Crackers with peanut butter and jelly or cheese spread or soup
- Canned vegetable or fruit
- Trail mix
- Canned juice, milk, coffee, or tea

Dinner

- Turkey or beef jerky and baked beans or canned chili
- Canned vegetables
- Canned fruit or pudding
- Canned juice, milk, coffee, or tea

Gallery
of Tools

In my work, I've found that using the right
organizing tools is the key to getting and
staying organized. That's why I include a list
of the tools you'll need with every project in
this book. In this section, you'll find some of
my favorite tools—but there are far too
many to show them all here! To see all the
tools I use and recommend, visit my website,
www.beverlyhillsorganizer.com

Ball holder

Bed elevators

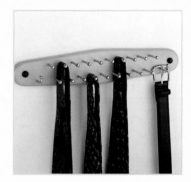

Belt and tie rack

Bike hoist

Bra box

Brief box

Bakeware rack

Canvas boxes

Clear ornament storage

Christmas tree
storage container

Click Clack food
storage containers

Corner shelf

Cupboard clips

Double hang

Drawer liner

Drawer doubler

Expandable shelf

Fishing pole holder

Fold 'n Stax

Jewelry drawer stacks

Kitchen island

Knife drawer organizer

Laundry hamper

Cabinet Carousel

Locker organizer

Media holder

Mirror valet (over the door)

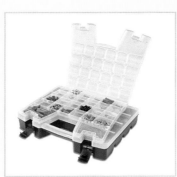

Portable storage container

Pull-out

Rafter solutions

Remote caddy

Shelf liner

Slide and Stack

Shoe rack (tilted)

Flatware drawer organizer

Slacks hanger

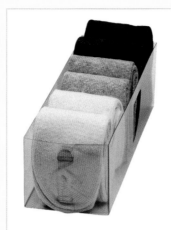

Sock box

Spice drawer organizer

Tension dividers

Tie box

Over-the-door towel holder

Undersink shelves

ADDITIONAL TOOLS (BY NAME ONLY)

2-Tier Lazy Susan

3-, 4-, and 6-Drawer chests

4-compartment box

64-Drawer organizer

6-compartment box

Acrylic drawer organizer

Acrylic flatware organizer

Baking soda caddy

Beverage dispenser

Bike stand

Bike wall mount

Blow dryer holder

Boot shapers

Canvas wardrobe

Canvass shelves

CD storage tray

China rack

Clear, jumbo, and large plastic containers

Comforter bag

Condiment caddy

Cord wrap

Cotton ball & swab holder

Deep storage basket

Desktop mail center

Dispenser 4, clear choice dispenser, ulti-mate dispenser

Drawer cubes

Dresser valet

DVD holder

Earring keeper

File crate

Freezer shelves

Frying pan rack

Garden kit, gardening organizer

Garment keeper

Garment wardrobe

Ironing center

Lid rack

Life Liner

Life liner

Light and garland box

Light wrap

Lipstick organizer

Long garment bag

Magazine holder

Mahogany drawer organizer

Mahogany utensil organizer

Medium and large stackable drawers

Medium and small helper shelves

Multi-purpose drawer organizer

Open top under bed storage

Ornament stackable drawers

Over rod garment bag

Over rod short bag

Paintbox

Paper bag holder

Parking guide

Pet food containers

Plastic baskets

Plastic file box

Plastic frunk

Plastic lid holder

Plastic storage

Reference file

Scrapbook organizer

Shovel holder

Slide & Stack

Slide-on cup & mug holders

Small, medium, large, and long stacking shelves

Sports center

Stackable audio cassette holder

Stackable CD holder

Stackable video holder

Stackable wine rack

Starter sets

Stemware holder

Storage basket

Storage cabinet

Towel and blanket bag

Undershelf placemat holder

Wall guard

Wall mounted drying rack

Wrap rack

Wrapping paper holder

Wreath box

Resources
for Home Organizing

Bed Bath & Beyond
110 Bi-County Boulevard, Suite114
Farmingdale, NY 11735
(800) 462-3966
www.bedbathandbeyond.com

The Beverly Hills Organizer
137 South Robertson Boulevard, #207
Beverly Hills, CA 90211
www.beverlyhillsorganizer.com

ClosetMaid
650 Southwest 27th Avenue
P.O. Box 4400
Ocala, FL 34474
(800) 227-8319
www.closetmaid.com

The Container Store
500 Freeport Parkway
Coppell, TX 75019
(888) 266-8246
www.containerstore.com

Home Depot
2455 Paces Ferry Road
Atlanta, GA 30339
1-800-430-3376
www.homedepot.com

IKEA
See website for the
store location nearest you
www.ikea-usa.com

Kmart
1-800 KMART4U
www.kmart.com

Linens-n-Things
866-568-7578
www.lnt.com

Office Max
(800) 283-7674
www.officemax.com

Organized Living
Corporate Headquarters:
5150 East Dublin-Granville Road
Westerville, OH 43081
(614) 918-2400
See website for the
store location nearest you
www.organizedliving.com

Pottery Barn
(888) 779-5176
www.potterybarn.com

Pottery Barn Kids
(800) 993-4923
www.potterybarnkids.com

Pottery Barn Teen
(866) 472-4001
www.pbteen.com

Staples
1-800-3STAPLE
www.staples.com

Target
Headquarters:
1000 Nicollet Mall
Minneapolis, MN 55403
(612) 304-6073
www.target.com

Wal-Mart
Wal-Mart Stores, Inc.
(800) WAL-MART
www.walmart.com

ACKNOWLEDGMENTS

* * * * * *

My gift of organizing others, and of teaching them how to organize for themselves, is truly my passion. Organizing has been my sanity and livelihood. Organizing is a form of therapy, which satisfies deep needs. The knowledge I share with you is my experience bestowed upon me from above. I have been blessed with the information in this book from the Lord. He has given me my purpose: to help you in helping yourself. It is my deepest desire to lead you on your path to your final goal—an organized existence.

There are many people who have supported me along my journey. I consider myself blessed beyond all my wildest dreams to know the following people and to call them friends. In alphabetical order: William Bayne, Shelly Berensen, Janet Brown, Mark Brunetz, Janette Cassandra, Bijan and Freyshtay Chadorchi, Jennifer Chadorchi, Debbie Chernoff, Beatrice Clancy, Stacey Cohen, Jay Cooper, Lawrence Davis, Tracey Dixon, Jeffrey Eget, Bonni Flowers, Dave Gross, Allen Lee Haff, Pastor Craig Henson, Beverly Holmes, Zoltan Jaeger, Cheryl Morgan, Kamran Naimi, Steve Nanini, Don and Niecy Nash, Woody Porch, Richard Pritzker, Herm Shulz, Kitty Stuart, Franck Verhaeghe, Mark Waldman, Marshal Wax, Peter Weinberger, Sharon and Bruce Williams, and Adrienne Zisser.

A very special person, dear friend, and loyal employee gave me the peace of mind I needed to pursue my career while I was raising my child. Thank you, Julia Rivas, for thirteen years of friendship, devotion, and love. I would not have been able to accomplish what I have done without you in our lives.

The photographs in this book were made possible by my brilliant photographer, Myk Mishoe, and the generosity of my clients and friends, who graciously opened their homes to our camera. In alphabetical order, I thank: Deborah Adri, Marni and Bob Battista, Catherine and Jeff Brown, Bijan and Freyshtay Chadorchi, Debbie and Larry Chernoff, Kari Dobson, Quinn and Bryan Ezralow, Grace and Jim Gray, Lisa and Mike Hansen, Michelle and Harold Henderson, Kathy and Randy Katz, Suzanne and Ric Kayne, jewelry designer Jack Kelege, Linda Krolop, Beth Morrison and Mike Singleton, Michele and Cary Shimohara, Tina Simon, and Brad Kimball and Steve Smelt.

Finally, a special thank you to my friends at E! Entertainment, Stephen Schwartz, Renee Simon, and Gina Rubinstein, for the incredible opportunity to do what I love to do, organize, on the Style Network's hit home makeover show, "Clean House."

Also Available from Quarry Books

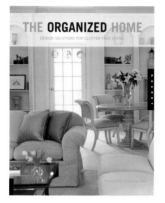

The Organized Home:
Design Solutions for Clutter-Free Living
By Randall Doll and Casey Ellis
ISBN:1-59253-018-4
$24.99 US, £16.99 UK
Hardcover; 160 pages
Available wherever books are sold

Designs that defeat disorder!

For most people, organization is not just an option, it's a necessity. With hectic lifestyles, computer passwords, frequent-flyer miles, an overload of information, and heaps of possessions, people are overwhelmed. They long to bring order into their chaotic, possession-filled lives. This book is the answer!

The Organized Home provides practical and inspirational advice for designing and maintaining an organized home. Filled with professional advice, hardworking information, and checklists that help you cut out the clutter, this book shows how your improved lifestyle will allow you to create the organized, peaceful, and beautiful home you crave!

Also Available from Fair Winds Press

Welcome Home:
Simple Tips for Turning Your House
into a Luxurious Retreat
By Melissa Placzek
ISBN:1-59233-056-8
$20.00
Hardcover; 108 pages
Available wherever books are sold

Turn your house into a spa retreat!

Every woman deserves a home that is welcoming, warm, and relaxing. In *Welcome Home*, Melissa Placzek gives you dozens of creative ways to make your home feel more like a spa. From decorating tips to spa recipes to memory making, this book holds the secrets to turning your house into a home.

With it's beautifully hand-lettered text and artful watercolors on every page, this book is a retreat all by itself. Relax and enjoy!

Melissa Placzek lives and works in Red Wing, Minnesota.

Also Available from Fair Winds Press

10-Minute Clutter Control:
Easy Feng Shui Tips for Getting
Organized
By Skye Alexander
ISBN:1-59233-068-1
$12.00
Paperback; 256 pages
Available wherever books are sold

The Feng Shui Cure For Clutter!

If you think that clutter is a fact of life, think again.
Feng shui-the ancient Chinese art of placement- can help
you organize every aspect of your life, both at home and the
office. With the simple tips & tricks in this book, you can
learn the secrets of this age-old clutter elimination system in
no time. Best-selling *10-Minute Feng Shui* author Skye
Alexander shows you how to transform your environment-
and in doing so, transform your life as well!

With *10-Minute Clutter Control*, you can throw out the bad,
organize the good, and attract the new luck, love, and
harmony that accompany a well-managed life.